Y0-CCJ-301

The Incredible

GIFTS

of Women

The Incredible GIFTS of Women

12 Gifts That Will

Change Your Life Now

Barbara Barrington Jones

DESERET BOOK
DISTRIBUTORS

To my dear departed husband
Hal Jones

A special thanks to Cindy Wilson, my dear friend, traveling companion
and scribe. This book would never have been written without her.

And to Janet Thomas, my patient, remarkably brilliant editor for over 20 years.

Special thanks to Suzanne Rodriguez, world-famous
composer and concert pianist, for allowing me to use her
incomparable music pro bono on the bonus CD.

I thank you all.

© 2008 Barbara Barrington Jones

ISBN 978-1-59038-923-2 (pbk.)

Printed in the United States of America

10   9   8   7   6   5   4   3   2   1

CONTENTS

Preface

WHY THIS BOOK?

I have traveled far and wide, speaking to thousands of women throughout the world. As I speak, I often ask for the women I meet to evaluate, on paper, the greatest problems they face in their daily lives. I receive varied answers that boil down to four major concerns:

- Too many women feel overwhelmed, overscheduled, and overtired
- Too many women don't like what they see in the mirror anymore
- Too many women are unhappy and/or depressed
- Too many women feel as if they are losing their spiritual connection with God and Jesus Christ

This book has been written in the hope that my experiences can help women who feel they have lost their God-given gifts of joy, happiness, and self-worth.

UNFORGETTABLE STORIES

Each chapter in this book opens by introducing a gift that we, as women, have been given by a loving Heavenly Father; and each chapter closes with an unforgettable story of one woman I have met in my travels. Most of the women you'll read about are not famous or well-known; in fact, their stories are not often known beyond their immediate families. They are women with quiet strength; and knowing how they made their journey—and succeeded—will inspire you.

I love and admire every woman I have met. They are courageous and extraordinary. I have laughed with them and cried with them as I have shared my story and listened to their stories. Each of us has our own set of problems, no matter what country we reside in and no matter what our circumstances: single, married, divorced, widowed. However, there are no "real" differences. We are all in this mortal journey together. We may have different colors of skin and speak different languages, but as my friend who is a Catholic nun said, "Though our choreography may be different, our dances are the same."

We are sisters in the gospel of Jesus Christ, and we were given incredible gifts associated with womanhood before we came to this earth. Our goal is to live our lives using these gifts in a positive, loving way to serve our Father in Heaven and our Savior Jesus Christ.

Chapter 1

THE GIFT OF DIVINE DESTINY

No matter your age or circumstance—college freshman, twenty-something working woman, middle-aged mother with six little children, widow, or wizened great-grandmother—your divine destiny lies ahead of you. God's plan for your life is constantly unfolding.

What will you do at that time? You must start thinking now. What are your gifts and talents? What does your patriarchal blessing say? It has been said, "If you could envision what God knows is possible for your life, you would rise up and never be the same again." I'd like you to read this letter I recently received that hits the point I would like to make in writing about this gift.

Dear Barbara,

I feel as though I have gone through a major personal transformation these past few days. This past fall, when the youngest of our 8 children left home to go away to school, I looked around me and I couldn't remember who I was! I was not the Laundry Queen, the Clutter Queen, the Homework Queen—you get the idea. I knew I was me somewhere inside, but I could not find myself. It reminded me of one of your quotes when you played your funny character, Melweena Dweeb: "If all is not lost, then . . . where is it?"

You said things during your women's conference that spoke to my soul. You told us that in order to discern our special talents and inclinations, we should think about the dreams and goals of our youth. The talents that we have discovered and developed. We should look for patterns in our lives: think about what is written in our patriarchal blessings, and notice the books that interest us the most when we go to the bookstore or library. You encouraged us all to think about our past accomplishments and experiences that brought us happiness and fulfillment in our lives. Those would be strong indicators of our special gifts. I realized that my passion is in the field of self-development.

Something clicked inside when you said, "It's not over until it's OVER!" I want to do many things during this earth life. Fear has held me back. But no more. From this moment on, I will not fear or doubt. I came home and wrote in my journal: "I will constantly be working on my goals, without hesitation, so that I will be prepared to do what I came here on earth to do, AND I WILL DO IT!" You helped me to realize that I actually can write the book I've dreamed of writing. I neglected to tell you that before I married I was an editor.

Blessings,

Cristie B. Gardner

"The Family: A Proclamation to the World" declares that we each have a divine destiny. The Young Women theme lists divine nature as one of seven values. And the very first words in the Relief Society declaration are, "We are beloved spirit daughters of God, and our lives have meaning, purpose, and direction" (*The Latter-day Saint Woman*, xi).

We are each unique and unequalled. No one will ever have your same destiny, just as no one will ever have your fingerprints. As you read how my destiny has taken shape, I hope you will be thinking of what experiences and revelations have made you who you are.

Unfortunately, the world also "teaches" us a number of things about our worth as women. And much of it is nothing more than a distraction to keep us from fulfilling our destiny as daughters of God. Two of the most dangerous distractions the world throws at women are self-comparison and a sense of inferiority. Couple these with the inevitable adversities in life, and you can have some major roadblocks to discovering who you really are.

Fortunately, as daughters of God, we have the tools to get past these distractions, to stop comparing ourselves to others, to embrace our status as children of a loving Heavenly Father, and to use our trials to make us better, not bitter.

A LETTER FROM HAL

Six months before my dear husband, Hal, passed away, he wrote the following letter and requested that I use it in this book to introduce my personal story—a story I share with the hope that you can learn from my adversities. Here is what he wrote:

*Hal is the person that Heavenly Father brought into
my life so that I could reach my divine destiny.*

Dearest Partner, Friend, and Wife,

We have been together for 29 years, and these are a few of
the beautiful things that I have observed that have made me
love and admire you more each year.

You are a woman who has suffered—one who has known
fear, abuse, and sadness, a woman who has known poverty, and
one, who when she finally "won" and saw a lifelong dream
coming true, gave up the "victory" in order to raise her son.

Together we have known happiness. We have raised two
children, and you have helped countless teenage girls and
women to change their lives for the better. I am grateful to
have been your partner in that endeavor also. You have been a
wonderful partner, best friend, and wife.

All my love always, Hal

When Hal wrote of fear, suffering, abuse, sadness, and poverty, he was referring to an abusive marriage I lived through for twelve years.

I was a ballerina. And the fear began when my husband took me off the stage in the middle of a ballet performance and bound my wrists, ankles, and mouth with surgical tape. He threw me into the car, pointed a shotgun at my legs, and threatened, "Now I'm going to blow your legs off so you can never dance again."

Despite his threats, I lived through several more years of suffering and sadness. Eventually, I got the courage to run away with my son to Atlanta, Georgia, where I joined the Atlanta Ballet Company. I later moved to Montreal. I couldn't get a full-time job with their dance company. I lived in a tenement house in one little room, and shared a bathroom with five other families. I slept on a couch, with my son beside me on some cushions on the floor. I walked to class every day in below-freezing weather with my three-year-old son holding my hand and walking beside me. I hardly had enough money for milk.

I finally gave up trying to survive on my own and returned to my abusive husband. I felt I had no choice. The fear and abuse continued. But I felt I had nowhere to go. The dream of my lifetime had been to go to Europe as a ballerina and dance in Paris. Shortly after returning to my husband from Montreal, I received a letter from a Canadian ballet company inviting me on their European tour. The itinerary included Paris— my dream come true! I soon learned, however, that I would be unable to take my son. So, I turned the opportunity down, giving up the thrill of a personal victory to raise my son.

We had another child, a daughter, for whom I am so grateful and love very much. To the world we appeared to be the perfect family of four. But I lived five more years in sheer terror, wondering where my husband had hidden a gun; he always had one nearby. One afternoon he walked into our living room, grabbed me by my hair and upper arm, and dragged me upstairs. He made me stand in the bathtub, pulled out a gun, and held it to my head. He said he was going to kill me and then kill himself. Tears streamed down my cheeks, and eventually my husband lowered the gun and left. Months later he took his own life.

THE BEGINNING OF A NEW LIFE

When I met Hal Jones, the dear, wonderful man who would become my second husband, I told him my story. He said, "Barbsie-bell, I think you better get right with God." I was thirty-one, and he was fifty-seven. I did as he said and attended mass at my Catholic church every day.

When Hal asked me to marry him, I left Dallas and my wonderful job there administrating a Barbizon fashion school for teenage girls and moved to San Francisco, California, to start a new life.

On my way to Dallas, I had a stopover in the El Paso airport, and my father came to see me. He brought me a book called *In the Presence of God,* which I read on the plane. At the end of the book was a prayer. It said, in essence, "Heavenly Father, I give you my past; I give my present; and I give you my future. I only want to do your will." I wrote the date, July 11, 1976, in the book along with my name. I had suffered through poverty, sadness, fear, and abuse. Now my life was to change, and my divine mission was about to commence.

Hal suggested that I read in Proverbs every day. I wanted to please him, so I tried to read them. But having never read the Bible, I could hardly understand a word. He then suggested I go to the local convent, where one of the nuns could teach me the Bible.

At the convent, my teacher was Sister Donna Marie. In our first lesson, she read to me from Isaiah 50:4–5, "The Lord God hath given me the tongue of the learned, that I should know how to speak a word in season to him that is weary: he wakeneth morning by morning, he wakeneth mine ear to hear as the learned.

"The Lord God hath opened mine ear . . ."

Little did I know that her inspired selections would lead me to my divine destiny.

My new life continued. I attended mass daily, but things were difficult. It was hard for me to be a full-time mother. I missed my job and the teenage girls that I so enjoyed working with. That was my passion and joy. I realized that I was a workaholic. Hal was gone half of the time, and I felt so lonely. Yes, I had my children, I went to PTA meetings, I was busy, but I missed working with those teenage girls. Hal was twenty-six years older than I and was by nature quite domineering. Although he was a remarkable man, I was beginning to think I had made a mistake and should return to Dallas and my old life.

FINDING JESUS CHRIST

While entertaining these thoughts of leaving, I attended mass. I was sitting in a pew toward the front, and the priest was reading a story from the New Testament. It was the story in Matthew about Christ walking on the water. When Peter saw the Savior walk on the water toward him, the Savior said to Peter, "Come," (Matthew 14:29).

I was only half-listening, absorbed in my own problems. Besides, I'm deathly afraid of water. But suddenly, I somehow felt I was in Peter's place. I felt that I was standing on the surface of the water, looking down. I could see greenish-black waves crashing all around me. As I started to take a step, I froze. To my horror, I felt myself sinking into the water, and it closing over my head. I felt the seaweed. I wanted to gasp for air but couldn't breathe. I truly believed I was drowning. Then I felt a strong hand encircle my wrist. I didn't see Him, but I knew it was the Savior lifting me up and out of the water. He seemed to say to my spirit, "Oh ye of little faith. Why did you doubt me? Do you think I would have bid you come all this way and not help you?"

When I opened the big wooden doors of St. Ignacious Church that day, I wondered if I had been dreaming. No! I felt like a person does when she climbs out of a swimming pool and the wind blows on her wet skin, cold and tingly. I knew something magnificent had happened to me. That day I felt as if I had been given a new start. The experience was so powerful that I wanted to remember it forever. I had been saved from a tragic mistake. I even went so far as to have a ring made with the inscription, "Oh, ye of little faith, why did you doubt me."

I couldn't wait to tell Sister Donna Marie about my experience. She read me a verse of scripture that said, "Except a man be born of water and of the Spirit, he cannot enter into the kingdom of God" (John 3:5). She told me that the water signifies rebirth.

Sister Donna Marie read me another verse that day: "I am the way, the truth, and the life: no man cometh unto the Father, but by me" (John 14:6).

I began a prayer that day that lasted five years. Every day I asked, "Jesus, who are you? Where are you?"

One summer, at the end of a vacation, my husband and I walked onto Temple Square in Salt Lake City and went to the visitors' center. As I walked in, they invited us to watch a movie about Joseph Smith, Moroni, and the golden plates. At the end of the film, there was a picture that I had never seen before. It was the Savior dressed in white robes looking directly at me with His arms outstretched. I so clearly heard Him say to my spirit, "Barbara, here I am. Come follow me." I sat there in the dark, with silent tears streaming down my cheeks. My prayer had been answered. It took three years for our family to be baptized in The Church of Jesus Christ of Latter-day Saints.

In 1984, I received my patriarchal blessing and was overwhelmed when I was told that through my efforts to learn, great treasures of knowledge would come to me. I received a blessing that I would increase in wisdom because of the many tender and special spirits who would come under my influence, some young and others older, and was promised that I would assist them to appreciate the beauty and wonder of the gospel of Jesus Christ. Others would seek my counsel, and I would guide and help them to meet and overcome their problems. I would be blessed to know their needs and how to assist them and help them acquire a knowledge of themselves and their importance to Heavenly Father. I was told I would be a means by which many would learn self-discipline in obedience to the commandments and to seek the principles that lead to eternal life. At the time, I didn't understand the meaning of all the phrases, but over the years, I began to see my divine destiny unfolding.

BECOMING A SPEAKER

Some time later, a girl in my ward who attended Brigham Young University and worked in the Continuing Education Department was asked if she knew of any female speakers that could join their youth outreach team. She suggested me, and I was called to come to BYU for an interview. I agreed even though inside I was saying, "Me, a speaker? Never! Don't they know I'm a ballerina?"

At the same time, I was the visiting teacher to the stake Relief Society president. She asked, "How would you like to give a talk for the women of the stake and tell them about your life?"

I was panic-stricken. Hal was not too thrilled that the women's conference was on Saturday. We had planned a ski trip that weekend, and he didn't want my speech to cut into his powder time. He begged me to give my talk, then leave right away so we could hit the slopes.

At the women's conference, I walked up to the podium. I was petrified and shaking. It was the last thing in the world I ever wanted to do. But I did it. Then I left immediately. We spent the weekend skiing and having a great time. But on every run, I rehearsed my speech of refusal for the BYU people. Then I started mentally making excuses to myself about why I could never do that sort of thing again.

On the last run of the day, I skied down the hill and met Hal. He said, "My leg is killing me." He reached down and pulled his pant leg up. His calf was swollen over his boot.

The doctor at the emergency hut took one look and said, "You have a blood clot, and if it breaks, it could either go to your heart and you'll have a heart attack, or it could go to your brain and you'll have a stroke." The ambulance came, and they rushed my husband, with me at his side, to the hospital.

In my ski jacket I had a little pocketbook copy of the Bible with me. The hospital instructed me to stay in the waiting room. I was sitting there thinking that I had already lost one husband to suicide, and I was not ready to lose another husband. I pleaded with the Lord, "Heavenly Father, I can't go through this again. Please, I'll do anything, but let him be okay."

I pulled the little Bible out of my pocket. It fell open to Isaiah 6:8–9, and I began to read. "Also I heard the voice of the Lord, saying, Whom shall I send, and who will go for us? Then said I, Here am I; send me.

"And he said, Go . . ."

I wondered how many of us had said these same words in the pre-mortal existence.

At that very moment, the doors opened and the doctor came in. "Mrs. Jones, we have good news for you. We have X-rayed your husband's leg, and there is nothing there."

I said, "I know."

And that was how I began the next part of my divine destiny as a speaker.

When I went to the interview at BYU, the first question they asked me was, "Sister Jones, do you have a testimony?"

I began to cry. "Yes, I have a testimony." I shared my testimony and feelings about Christ and the Church, and then I was asked to do a series of summer youth conferences.

Even though I was now a speaker, and an official employee of BYU, I had what to me was a difficult and unsolved question. I wondered why we couldn't pray directly to Jesus. Yes, I knew that this was Christ's church. But Jesus was the one I had prayed to for five years, asking, "Who are you? And where are you?" It was more difficult for me to pray to Heavenly Father. I didn't feel like I had a relationship with Him as I did with my Savior. I didn't know my Heavenly Father.

At that point I really didn't realize that understanding the gospel is a process, and that understanding the purpose of our earthly mission will take many years. Our divine destiny will be revealed to us through our pain and adversity, through inspiration from the Holy Ghost, through prayer, through the temple and the scriptures and our patriarchal blessings, and the many other marvelous experiences God gives to us.

GOING INTO THE WORLD

About ten years later I was asked by a sister at BYU's Education Week to come to Australia to speak in her stake. While there, one of the Relief Society sisters in Australia asked me to send a resume to her office at a local bank. I had my office fax it over. I assumed it was for another Relief Society event; but this sister wanted me to speak to the women at the bank! Well, it was one thing for me to go to a Relief Society social, where I could talk about God, but speaking in the world was more than intimidating.

Fortunately, my husband encouraged me to tell her yes, and he even hired a business agent to start promoting me in Australia. I was shocked when I saw my itineraries. I was booked to do the valedictory address at the University of Queensland; then it was a lecture at a leading law firm; a speech to a private Catholic girls' school and convent; a lecture at a mortgage banking business and another to the management of a respected hotel. I was a nervous wreck. I lost every bit of confidence, and my self-esteem plummeted. All I could think was, "I'm going to stand there in front of all those people and make a fool of myself. I am definitely not a professional speaker."

FINDING MY HEAVENLY FATHER

My husband sensed my shaken confidence and decided to try to divert my mind from the situation. He invited some friends to accompany us to Los Angeles to see a revival of the classic Broadway musical, *Showboat*. It was a fabulous production. Having spent years in the theatre as a dancer, I was enthralled. The singing, the dancing, the sets, the costumes, every moment was spellbinding. It certainly took my mind off all my fears.

The story is of a riverboat called *Showboat*. At every port where the showboat docked, people of that town would come to see the show. The captain and his wife had a lovely daughter with a beautiful voice who performed in the show. She fell in love with a riverboat gambler, and they were married and moved away to Chicago. He, however, was only happy and successful when he gambled and won big. So most of their life they lived in poverty. Her parents received letters, but she never told them the truth of her sad marriage. Finally, after many years, her mother and father decided to visit her. They didn't know that her husband had left her. She was alone and trying to start over. A friend told her to come to the dinner theatre where he worked and audition as a singer. She took his advice but didn't do well. Her voice was shaky. She had definitely lost her confidence. She didn't get the job. But on New Year's Eve, the dinner theatre's star quit unexpectedly, and the management was forced to call her to fill in.

As the scene opens, the parents arrive in Chicago. It's New Year's Eve. The mother decides to stay in the hotel and rest, but the father puts on his tuxedo and goes out for the night. As he walks the streets, he decides on a place with dinner and entertainment. Unknown to him, this is the dinner theatre where his daughter will be appearing.

As the patrons are finishing their desserts and ordering more champagne, the show begins. His daughter's name is announced. She walks out in a beautiful red velvet gown, holding a fan of red ostrich plumes. She starts to sing. Her voice is beautiful but weak. She is terrified. Some intoxicated patron starts chanting to get her off the stage. The entire audience joins in. The poor girl, standing alone, continues to sing with a voice that weakens with each note.

Suddenly, her father stands, and, with conviction, walks boldly to the front of the stage, thrusting both arms into the air in a dramatic gesture of silence. A hush falls over the audience as he says in a powerful and deep voice, "Shhh, don't you know, that's my daughter!"

At that moment in the show, I had the most incredible spiritual experience. I was being taught spirit to spirit. My Heavenly Father seemed to be saying to me, "I am sending you out into the world. Don't be afraid. Whenever you stand to speak, I will be right there with you. I will stand before you and tell everyone, 'Shhh, don't you know, that's my daughter!'"

I just sat there with tears streaming down my face. For the first time in some fifty-odd years, I knew that I had a Heavenly Father who loved me. I thought, "Who am I that my Heavenly Father loves me and knows my heart, my fears, my insecurities, my questions, that He would let me know that I am His daughter? He truly loves me, and even if I go into the world, He will be there with me."

Several months later, I flew to Australia. At my first speaking event, which was the valedictory address at the University of Queensland, there were dinner plates rattling, wine glasses clinking, and a hundred people chatting. After the dinner a formal welcome was given, and they introduced me as the speaker. As I walked to the podium, I felt a hush fall over the audience. He was there! I knew my Heavenly Father was standing in front of me saying, "Shhh, don't you know, that's my daughter!"

BLESSINGS

Some time later, I told this story at a women's conference, after which I received this letter:

Dear Sister Jones,

There once was a not-so-pretty, chubby little girl, afraid of life and all it had to offer. All her life she was too afraid to try much of anything, because whatever she did, no matter how hard she tried, she was always second. There was always someone prettier, smarter, thinner, faster, more creative, more spiritual. Her self-esteem plummeted as the years marched on and on. She struggled and struggled. Who was she? . . .

This was the very question you asked the sisters of my stake. At least it looked like you standing at the podium, but somehow it didn't sound like your voice. To me it seemed as if the Lord Himself stood before me and spoke the seven most beautiful words my earthly ears have ever heard: "Shhh, don't you know, she's my daughter."

Suddenly I knew who I was. All the uncertainty and self-doubt lifted away, and my spirit seemed to jump right out of its shell and yell, "Oh, yeah, silly me. I almost forgot."

How can I explain to you the freedom I feel that I have been given? You reminded me that I am never alone. He was there with me all the time. Every time I needed Him. Even though I didn't ask for His help. He didn't care that I wasn't beautiful or that I sang off-key or couldn't play the piano or dance. Despite all my earthly limitations, I was suddenly beautiful. I was second to none, and even though there were hundreds of sisters there today and millions of others on the earth and more in the spirit world, I realized that I was first. We are all first. We are all His daughters.

Sheri Dew said, "There is nothing more vital to our success and happiness here than learning to hear the voice of the Spirit. It is the Spirit who reveals to us our identity, which isn't just who we are but who we have always been. And when we know that, our lives take on a sense of purpose so stunning we can never be the same again" ("Knowing Who You Are—And Who You've Always Been," 278).

He *is* there. And we are His daughters—you are His daughter.

My hope in sharing my experience is that you can take it and apply the lessons I received to your own life, that whenever you lose your confidence, whenever you have difficulties and can't cope with life's challenges, you'll remember that He is with you and stands before you in every situation, saying, "Shhh, don't you know, she's my daughter."

I encourage you to learn this for yourself by going back through your life and writing your own autobiography. What experiences have made you who you are? Describe them. Sometimes our greatest treasures can be found in the adversities of our lives. We've heard it said, "No pain, no gain," and I believe that pain and adversity can bring gain. Real pain can bring to us genuine love and humility, if we so choose. We can find within pain an unequaled and remarkable passion to help others in similar circumstances. It is through those painful experiences that God teaches us the wisdom we must learn in order to fulfill our life's mission.

Write down the scriptures that have meant the most to you. Write down your most spiritual experiences. How did you come to know God and Jesus Christ? Take out your patriarchal blessing, analyze each sentence, and study it. Go to a bookstore and see what subjects you are drawn to.

My divine destiny is still unfolding. My dreams, which my husband spoke of in his introductory letter in this chapter, have become a reality. Together we have known happiness, raised our children, and have helped countless teenage girls and women to change their lives for the better.

Had it not been for the twelve years of abuse, I would never have had the passion that I do to help women and young women. This is my life's work—to serve my Father in Heaven and His Son, Jesus Christ.

It has been said that we view life narrowly, as through a hole in a fence, while God is overhead surveying the entire panorama. When we understand His perspective, it widens ours, and we come closer to living our lives and fulfilling our divine destiny.

Napua Kalama TeNgaio Baker

NAPUA'S STORY

I met Napua Kalama TeNgaio Baker more than twenty years ago at BYU–Hawaii. We have been good friends ever since. She and her sister, Theresa, even flew to San Francisco to be with me during Hal's funeral. She is the most beautiful, gracious woman that I have ever known and one who truly emanates the pure love of Christ. Yet, her life has been filled with challenges, trials, and tribulations. She once said to me, "I would have never dreamed that a poor little girl from the island of Molokai would ever become the vice-president of BYU–Hawaii. I never aspired to this job. I did not feel qualified, but I knew I could do it because it was my mission, my divine destiny."

Napua was born to sunshine and palm trees on the Hawaiian island of Molokai, where her grandfather had worked in the leper colony. This is her story:

My family's first home was a little wooden frame house just across from the chapel next to the coconut grove. We played in the coconut grove near the beach. The beach had muddy waters, but we swam there anyway. At night we'd go fishing, go to our neighbor's home, and eat poi out of their family's poi bowl.

My parents were "doers." They ran a school bus service, a taxi service, a corner service station, and a tour guide business. That took a lot of initiative. My mom knew the value of work, taught us all not to be afraid of work, and to have a strong work ethic. My father was a visionary man who encouraged me to go to college. He had only completed the ninth grade. My mother hadn't finished high school either. But they shared a vision for us children.

My sister, Theresa, and I graduated from Kamehameha High School. I studied at Church College of Hawaii (now Brigham Young University–Hawaii) where I met my future husband, Michael TeNgaio. I transferred to BYU in Provo. Michael soon followed, and we were married in the Manti Utah Temple. I worked at BYU's Continuing Education Office, and my husband and I attended school.

After I graduated from BYU in elementary education, we returned to Hawaii with our son, Lance. We settled down in Laie, and I took a teaching job in a neighboring town.

After ten years of marriage, my husband became ill. I had to leave my job to care full-time for him and the children. I stayed home for five years, and during those years I learned independence and self-reliance. I had married a man who was now mentally ill and suicidal. He would drive 100 miles an hour with us in the car. Eventually, he was institutionalized in his homeland of New Zealand. We were poor and on welfare. Since I had given up my teaching job, I went to work on the Church farm for $4 per hour. I had prayed about this decision and, since it was only temporary, I would make the best of it. Relief Society was my anchor through my trials. I would attend alone and feel the love of the sisters. I gained strength from them.

I made the decision to go to Provo to graduate school. My three children and I moved in with my sister, Theresa, and her five children in Provo. I completed my graduate program in only fifteen months. The same month my son, Lance, left on his mission to Japan, I received my master's degree.

BYU–Hawaii asked me to return as the director of Continuing Education. At home again in Laie, I tried to bring my husband back to Hawaii three times. But each time the doctor said, "No!" My husband remained in New Zealand in the environment and care he needed. We eventually divorced.

A few years later, I met a visiting professor and recent convert, John Baker. Our friendship blossomed, and we were married in the Laie Hawaii Temple. He was a very caring and wonderful man, but the unimaginable happened. My new husband passed away unexpectedly during heart surgery when a blood clot moved to his brain. I was grateful for the short time we had together and grateful for the companionship of the Holy Ghost to comfort me during this time. Only three months earlier, I had been asked to be a seminary teacher. As I learned the scriptures, I learned the companionship of the Holy Ghost. I knew once again I must press forward in faith.

Three years later, I started having pains in my jaw. I went to the dentist, had root canals, and still had pain. The pain went up my cheek. I started to lose my memory. A neurologist suggested an MRI; the headaches and loss of memory continued. I was notified that the MRI had shown a tumor in my brain the size of an orange. Shock! I was told to put my affairs in order as I prepared for surgery. If I happened to survive, I could expect to have permanent handicaps of intellect and senses. If the tumor was malignant, I could expect radical, debilitating treatment to follow.

I faced the greatest challenge of my life. Before surgery, the doctor told me to go and have a week of joy with my family. Many prayers were said on my behalf. In the hospital conference room I gathered with my family before surgery and was given a priesthood blessing. In the blessing I was told that "angels would guide the hands of the neurosurgeon, and my surgery would be successful." I read my patriarchal blessing before leaving that room. My blessing promised me a mind that is keen and alert. It also counseled me, "Do not despair. Every obstacle can be surmounted with the help of the Lord. Once it is surmounted then you will go forward with new vision and determination."

I knew I would be all right—that my mission was not over. After what was supposed to be a 13½-hour surgery, they found, within only seven hours, that the tumor was benign, and they were able to remove it completely. I came out of the surgery with no permanent disabilities. My prayers had been answered, and promises fulfilled.

Being a university vice president is not something I sought after. But since my surgery, I realize the Lord put me here to build up the kingdom. I am here today because in my heart I would do anything for Heavenly Father and His Son, Jesus Christ. And everything I do is for Him in order to fulfill my mission—my divine destiny—here on earth.

I would never have believed that while recovering from my surgery I would be called as the stake Relief Society president. I was concerned about my strength and ability to do the work, but when I prayed my answer came, "Have faith, and trust me." It's a joy to me, more so since *my surgery, and because of my increased love for the Savior, and gratitude to Him, that I have more love to give to my family and to the students.*

So why do we have trials, tribulations, illnesses? How many of us would volunteer for such afflictions? Illnesses are not punishments that God sends to us. Things happen to us in this life. We have imperfect, immortal bodies. We are susceptible to sickness, not as a punishment from God but as a natural result of mortality. We can learn lessons from physical illness and challenges. My illness helped me to focus on the Savior and the feelings in my heart.

I thank the Lord for every challenge, trial, and tribulation in my mortal journey that has humbled me to submissiveness, helped me to listen to the promptings of the Holy Ghost, directed me to search for answers in the scriptures and from the counsel of our past and living prophets and apostles, and to get on bended knees to express gratitude and seek guidance in sincere prayer. This has increased my faith in Him and in His power to perform miracles. It has helped me to work through trials without fear, as President Spencer W. Kimball teaches us in Faith Precedes the Miracle: *"Is there not wisdom in God giving us trials that we might rise above them, responsibilities that we might achieve, work to harden our muscles, sorrows to try our souls? Are we not exposed to temptations to test our strength, sickness that we might learn patience, death that we might be immortalized and glorified?"*

The answer is a definite, "Yes!"

When Alton Wade became the President of BYU–Hawaii, he asked Napua to be the administrative assistant to the president. President Wade said, "She had all the qualities I was looking for: intelligence, loyalty, and a commitment to service. She was just as gentle as she could be, but didn't back away from making the tough decisions. In 1993, I had the great honor of appointing Napua Baker as the first female vice president in the history of the Church."

Have you thought about your purpose in life, your divine destiny? Go to the mountains. Pray and listen. Take your patriarchal blessing. Find the magnitude within it. Try to understand. Study and feast upon the words of Christ. Be grateful. Be humble.

May your life be filled with joy and peace that flows from doing the will of a loving Heavenly Father and His Only Begotten Son, Jesus Christ. May you have the constant companionship of the Holy Ghost to guide, edify, uplift, and inspire you to realize your divine destiny.

Chapter 2

THE GIFT OF
CELESTIAL TRAITS

Elder Robert E. Wells said, "I am convinced that women are special creatures, true angel daughters of our Heavenly Father, and that they arrive from heaven itself trailing clouds of glory earned through their premortal faithfulness and valiance, endowed with spiritual gifts and talents that are different and, in many ways, superior to those of men. Women have an advantage over men that is obvious. Men tend to think with their brilliant minds. Women, on the other hand, have an advantage in that they have equally brilliant minds, with sweet and tender hearts and God-given instincts necessary to bring children into this world, nurture and raise them" ("Wonderful Women in My Life," BYU—Hawaii Women's Conference, August 1997.)

In "The Family: A Proclamation to the World," it says, "All human beings—male and female—are created in the image of God. Each is a beloved spirit son or daughter of heavenly parents, and, as such, each has a divine nature and destiny. Gender is an essential characteristic of individual premortal, mortal, and eternal identity and purpose" (*Ensign,*

November 1995, 102). By divine design, Heavenly Father made us male and female. I believe that Heavenly Father's greatest gift to us was that of being a woman, whose major role it is to nurture and to love. This role does not depend on a woman's circumstances. It does not depend on whether you are single, married, widowed, or have never had a child. We each have been given countless gifts in order to fulfill our divine feminine destiny. Within this chapter you will find at least thirty of the gifts often granted to women, but we will discuss just a few.

You may not have all of these, but it's likely you have at least a few of them: a desire to learn and grow, the ability to think with your emotions, sensitivity, a desire to nurture relationships, quiet strength, femininity, a giving heart, and a strong sense of intuition.

A Desire to Learn and Grow. Women like to study, learn, and grow. I once heard it said that the majority of LDS books are purchased by women. I also know from personal experience that the majority of people attending Education Week are women. I know from experience that women are note takers. We also like to delve and discover, learning ways to help ourselves and others. We take classes and workshops on a wide range of subjects, including cooking, finance, home decorating, computer technology, languages, strengthening the family, and parenting. I recently met a woman who decided to go back to college once all of her children were in school. She received her teaching degree and is thrilled with her first third-grade class!

Your love of learning may be one of the reasons you are reading this book.

The Ability to Think With Your Emotions. My sister, Dr. Paula Hall, a family therapist, says that women think with their emotions, which allows us to remember a tremendous amount of feelings and details.

That's why we remember the details of important events. We remember what we wore on a first date, what music was playing, and what we ate. Men tend to be more logical and factual and remember how much it cost. It doesn't make it less important to them; it's just the difference in how we attach our memories.

Sister Camilla Eyring Kimball wrote in her journal of the day she met her future husband, Spencer: "One evening soon after school began, I had stayed at school for a faculty meeting and was standing on Thatcher's Main Street, waiting for the jitney bus, when Spencer Kimball came along. He introduced himself and said he was going by bus to Pima to visit a friend. We sat together on the bus and discussed Shakespeare and similar highbrow subjects, each hoping to impress the other. I was wearing a white voile dress with blue design. I had made the dress over and wished I were wearing something nicer. He wore white socks, but I forgave him. In Pima he walked me home from the bus and asked if he might call on me sometime. That weekend he invited me to his sister Helen's birthday party, but I had to go to Duncan on a Sunday School stake board visit and couldn't go with him" (in Caroline Eyring Miner, *Camilla*, 60).

Of the same event, President Kimball wrote in his journal: "Met Camilla Eyring and accompanied her on the bus to her home. Asked her out."

Sensitivity. Women are innately sensitive. When scientists scanned the brains of men and women as they recalled emotional experiences, it was discovered that the sexes respond differently. Sad feelings activated neurons in an area of the brain eight times larger in women than in men (see Hales, "If You Think We Think Alike, Think Again," 110).

Author Dianne Hales reports: "The female brain also may detect other's emotions more accurately. Dr. Raquel Gur, a neuropsychiatrist at the University of Pennsylvania, and her husband, psychologist Ruben Gur, did brain scans on volunteers who viewed photographs of actors depicting various emotions. Both sexes knew happiness when they saw it, but the men had a much harder time recognizing sadness in women. 'A woman's face had to be really sad for a man to see it'" ("If You Think We Think Alike, Think Again," 110). Apparently, the women could look at a picture and recognize immediately even the beginnings of sadness.

A Desire to Nurture Relationships. For many women, good relationships are foremost in their minds. If there are troubles in any relationship—God, self, husband, children, extended family, or friends—they can feel unsettled.

Most mothers would agree with this common saying: "We are only as happy as our saddest child." This is, of course, because our lives—and therefore our emotions—are so intertwined with the people we love.

We, as women, are relational to everything, not just people. Even the way young girls carry their books down the hall is personal and relational. Girls tend to put an arm around the books and hold them close to the heart—just as they would a child.

A man is more objective. He holds a book at arm's length.

For women it is unsettling if the washing machine is broken down, the screen door needs repair, or a child's room is in disarray. All these things are a part of her life. They are personal and relational to her.

Quiet Strength. In his book, *The Mount and the Master,* Elder Robert E. Wells writes: "I once visited a 100,000-acre ranch [in Argentina] where the owner . . . was raising and training thoroughbred horses to be used for racing, polo, and for use on the ranch. . . . The ranch had over one thousand of these beautiful animals, each with its pedigree, each well trained or in the process. The ranch's reputation was such that there was a demand for its horses all over the world at premium prices.

"I asked the owner if we would be able to see a rodeo . . . in which the *gauchos,* would break horses. He was aghast. 'Not on this ranch you won't!' was his emphatic response. 'Since our horses . . . have to be lightning fast, fearless, and courageous on the playing field, instantly obedient to every hint of a command and superbly maneuverable, we would never "break" a horse—we do not want to break his spirit. We love our horses and we work patiently with them until they are *manso.*' *Manso* means meek, but here was a new meaning for the word. He explained, 'Our *manso* horses are full of fire and spirit, but they are obedient and well trained.'

"So meek can mean obedient and well trained, an added spiritual application to the words of the Savior. The Savior did not mean for us to be doormats—he certainly was not one. Rather, I think he meant that we should be obedient and well-trained. We can be strong, enthusiastic, talented, spirited, zealous, and bold, and still be meek—obedient and well trained—and able to coexist in the success-oriented world in which we live" (29).

I believe that most women are *manso*—we possess a quiet strength that affects everyone around us. We are talented, spirited, zealous, and bold—but still meek.

President James E. Faust wrote of his wife, Ruth, "In my long life I have found peace, joy, and happiness beyond my hopes and dreams. One of the supreme benedictions in my life has been my marriage to an elect daughter of God. I love her with all my heart and soul. Upon the wind of her spirit have my wings been carried. We were married in the Salt Lake Temple 57 years ago when I was a soldier in World War II and did not know if I would come back alive. Her strong, unwavering faith and support have strengthened my own testimony in times of challenge and difficulty. My inevitable eternal journey, if I am so favored, will be wonderful with her at my side" ("A Growing Testimony," *Ensign,* November 2000, 54). I am certain that all the men who preside over this Church are backed up by women like Ruth Faust—women with quiet strength.

Femininity. Somehow the focus of many women in the world has changed over the past few decades as they have tried to become equal with men. In striving to do so, some of the natural abilities and contributions that we as women are blessed with have become lost.

How blessed we are that we are feminine women. What a magnificent gift. We need never be ashamed of or try to be different than that which we were created to be. President James E. Faust observed, "[Femininity] is the divine adornment of humanity. It finds expression in your capacity to love, your spirituality, your sympathy, delicacy, radiance, sensitivity, creativity, charm, graciousness, gentleness, dignity, and quiet strength. It is manifest differently in each girl or woman, but each of you possesses it. Femininity is part of your inner beauty" ("Womanhood: The Highest Place of Honor," *Ensign,* May 2000, 96).

A Giving Heart. We are blessed to be true angel daughters of our Father in Heaven. As the hymn, "As Sisters in Zion," says,

> *The errand of angels is given to women;*
> *And this is a gift that, as sisters, we claim:*
> *To do whatsoever is gentle and human,*
> *To cheer and to bless in humanity's name.*
> (*Hymns, no. 309*)

It is in a woman's nature to be giving and compassionate.

In the national news, I read a beautiful story of a most giving woman, a seventy-six-year-old schoolteacher named Annette Swann from Ft. Stewart, Georgia. Every day this teacher shared her lunch with a tall, young black boy who other teachers often blamed for any trouble that took place in the area. Swann's daughter said, "Mama wasn't having any of that! She was his champion!" That young boy turned out to be three-time NBA champion, Shaquille O'Neal, who never forgot his fourth-grade teacher's kindness, and honored her several years ago in an NBA game (see "Shaq Jumps at Chance to Thank His Teacher," USA *Today,* April 11, 2006).

Elder Neal A. Maxwell said, "In our modern kingdom, it is no accident that women were, through the Relief Society, assigned compassionate service. So often the service of women seems instinctive, while that of some men seems more labored. . . . So often our sisters comfort others when their own needs are greater than those being comforted. That quality is like the generosity of Jesus on the cross. Empathy during agony is a portion of divinity. . . .

"When the real history of mankind is fully disclosed, will it feature the echoes of gunfire—or the shaping sound of lullabies? The great armistices made by military men—or the peacemaking of women in homes and in neighborhoods? Will what happened in cradles and kitchens prove to be more controlling than what happened in congresses? When the surf of the centuries has made the great pyramids so much sand, the everlasting family will still be standing. . . . The women of God know this" ("The Women of God," in *Woman,* 95–96).

A Strong Sense of Intuition. A woman I met in South Africa once shared this with me: "My son is grown and studying to be an accountant.

He gets up early—4:00 AM—studies, and takes classes. He has to drive an hour to get to class.

"One morning I woke up at 7:30 AM, sat up in bed, and I felt like something bad was happening. I fell to my knees and said, 'Heavenly Father, please protect my son.' I prayed with all my heart and stayed there on my knees for fifteen or twenty minutes.

"That evening I called my son and asked him where he was at 7:30 that morning.

"He said, 'Mom, I was on my way to class, and I fell asleep at the wheel. I was getting ready to go over an embankment, and I suddenly woke up at that moment and slammed on the brakes. I looked down at the clock and it was 7:30 AM.'

"I told him I was praying for him."

I remember having a strikingly similar experience. One morning, at 6:00 AM, I sat straight up in bed and said, "Something is wrong with John."

My husband said, "John? He's on a mission in Argentina."

I said, "I know, but something is wrong."

Then my husband tried using psychology. "Don't you trust Heavenly Father?"

I responded, "I am John's mother."

I started by calling the MTC, and within half an hour I reached the mission home in Argentina. The person on the phone said, "Sister Jones, how did you know?"

"How did I know what?"

"About Elder Jones. He's up in the hills of Méndoza. He has appendicitis, and there's not a hospital up there!"

How did I know? I just knew!

It turned out to be an amazing experience. He made it to the mission home and was given a priesthood blessing. He did not have to be operated on and has never had any further problems with his appendix.

Never forget that no matter where you are in life: single, married, childless, widowed, or divorced, we are His daughters and brought these feminine heavenly gifts with us when we came to earth. If you never have the opportunity to raise a child, it does not exclude you from the satisfaction and fulfillment of touching the lives of children with your caring and tender love. You can use your gift of nurturing in a myriad of ways that will not only bless your life but will certainly bless the lives of everyone around you.

I met Sue when she was a stake Relief Society president. In my talk to the sisters that day I had spoken about the miracle of co-partnership with God in clothing His spirit children with physical bodies. Then I shared the story of a sister I had met who had spent years of unhappiness, depression, and devastation because she was unable to bear children.

One night she had a dream. She was sitting in a council of women in heaven. Heavenly Father said, "I have some children who I am sending to earth whose mothers will be unable to raise them. These children are precious to me. Which one of you will raise them for me?"

She said that she saw herself literally leap to her feet, shoot her stretched waving hand into the air, and enthusiastically say, "I WILL! I WILL!" That dream changed her life. She realized that there were special children waiting for just her.

After I shared this story and the meeting was over, Sue drove me back to my hotel. During the drive, she shared her story, which I reprint here with her permission.

Sue Alder's Story

As a young girl I would say that I wanted to be a walking baby factory. When Darryl and I got married, having children was a priority. It soon became evident that it wasn't going to be easy. To many it appeared as though we were delaying our family. I went

The Alder Family

through some very depressing times. I didn't want to be with women who were pregnant because it just reminded me of my inadequacies. All conversations inevitably turned to children or childbirth and labor. People asked questions like, "Why don't you have any kids?" My bishop said, "Don't you think it's about time you start a family?" We had started on a seemingly endless twelve-year journey of fertility drugs, surgeries, and shots.

Finally we decided to pursue adoption. Since my patriarchal blessing said, "You will have sons and daughters," I did everything in my power to make it come to pass. A friend, who worked for LDS Family Services and knew we were anxious to adopt, called us to say he had a birth mother looking for parents who were active LDS, temple recommend holders, and college educated. He asked if we would like to hurry and apply?

Ha! I hand carried and delivered our paper work to the office that day!

That same day I had a divine intuitive experience. My husband and I attended the temple. After the session, I walked to the door of a sealing room that adjoined and looked in. I had the overwhelming feeling that I would bring a baby back to be sealed to me in this room. I felt calm as I rode home that night. Little did I know that two days later that very special baby would be born.

After Thanksgiving our caseworker called to ask if we had heard anything. We had not. He said if that was the case, we were not going to get this baby. We submerged our sorrows by going out and spending the money we had set aside to buy things for the baby.

A week later our caseworker called again and said, "I have a Christmas present for you! It's a baby boy! He will be there at 6:00 this evening." When we hung up, we both laughed and cried and hugged and laughed and cried some more. That evening as they brought baby Nicholas in and put him in my arms, they said "Merry Christmas!" Yes, this was going to be the best Christmas ever!

When Nick was six months old and his adoption was legally finalized, we took him to the temple to be sealed together as an eternal family. We were sitting in the sealing room, and I had a sudden recollection. This was the very room I had peeked into the night I got the inspiration that I would be bringing a baby back.

We were aching to have more children. Little did I know that it would take seven more years, with four adoptions falling through. Then one day, out of the blue, Darryl's brother felt strongly that he should send us a large sum of money for adoption. He didn't want finances to stand in our way. Unbelievable!

Shortly after, our doctor called to say that he knew a young woman who needed to place her baby for adoption. The baby would be bi-racial. Was I interested? It took me all of two seconds to say, "Yes."

When they called us to come to the hospital, they told us it was a girl. Standing outside the nursery window, the nurse mouthed the words, "Do you want to hold her?" A few moments later I was holding her in my arms.

She was the most beautiful newborn baby I had ever seen. Yet, I still couldn't allow myself the luxury of feeling too much because I was so afraid something would happen and I would lose her.

As we drove home, I could smell her on my hands. I didn't want to wash them. Darryl and I felt nervous about whether this was really all going to work out. Unless you have been through the adoption process, it's hard to understand what an emotional roller coaster the entire thing can be.

Finally the call came that we could pick her up. Darryl, Nick, and I went to the hospital. As I stood there alone wondering what was going on, I almost got physically ill. I was so scared that something had gone wrong. Finally a nurse came out, "Well, Mom, are you ready?" She ushered me in and I started to cry. I was standing and crying and changing her into the clothes that we brought for her to wear home when I was given a teddy bear from her birth parents and a letter that the birth mother had written: "To our baby girl." Even though I was so happy about getting a baby, I was keenly aware that before this could happen, another mother had to say good-bye. Six months later we took Ashley to the temple to be sealed to us. It was a miraculous day! It seemed that day that the heavens opened, and the angels rejoiced!

Two years after adopting Ashley, we felt it was "that time" again. Our attorney knew a young mother who was carrying a bi-racial baby and asked if we would be interested in pursuing the adoption. "Of course," I said. I immediately wrote a letter to the mother about how we felt about adoption and having a mixed-race family. I was told that my letter had touched her and that she wanted us to adopt her baby. On Father's Day, the birth grandmother called, "You said that you wanted a boy, and it is a little boy."

It was a memorable Father's Day for us all. We would name him Austin. When we picked him up, the nurse was so cute! She treated me just like I had been the natural mother. She made a special wristband for me and even made me sit in a wheelchair as I held my new baby and she wheeled me out. It was great!

The evening Austin was sealed to us in the temple, six months later, was a sweet and precious experience on a calm and peaceful snowy night.

The next few years were busy and happy, but I felt that our family was still not complete. I was tired of the adoption roller coaster, and I knew that God could do anything. If He wanted me to have children naturally then it could be. I even had Darryl give me blessings, and I would tell him what I thought he should say. We were building a house when I started having horrible cramps. I had been pregnant about eight weeks and miscarried. I felt that if it happened once, it could happen again. A few days later at a luncheon my friend said that she had wanted to do things her way and was not listening to the Spirit and nothing was going right. But when she gave in and turned things over to the Lord, everything fell into place. It was like a dagger to my heart! In my mind I apologized to Heavenly Father for the way I had acted. I told Him that if there was another baby that needed a mother I would do whatever it took.

That night, that very night, the lady who had brought me home from the luncheon called to tell me that she knew of a baby coming available and asked if Darryl and I were interested? "Yes!" She gave me a number, and the process started.

The day after we met the birth mother I woke up with the name Hayley in my head. Of course there were many, many obstacles from that day until we went to pick her up at the hospital. We were told that we couldn't take her home until she kept her formula down. We decided to stay at a hotel next to the hospital.

The next morning the doctor came in and asked us how many children we had? We told him three. Then he smiled at us and said, "And you got up all night to do the feedings?" Darryl told him yes. The doctor then commented that he thought we knew what were doing and he released her into our care.

The hardest part was yet to come. I had never had to watch a birth mother say good-bye before. I probably cried more than anyone. Her mother was there, as were her sister and her two-year-old son. It tore my heart out to look out the car window and watch the expressions on each face as we drove away.

Hayley's adoption was finalized. In the car on the way to the temple to be sealed, Nick said to his siblings, from his vast amount of experience, "This will be the neatest experience! You'll love it!"

Having a baby in the house again after six years was great. Nick, who was almost sixteen, would come home after school and say, "Where's my baby?" Ashley loved having a sister even though she was eight years younger, and Austin continued being kind and gentle to her and would sit and talk to her in her baby seat. Darryl and I felt content.

I thank my Father in Heaven for teaching me that He had special children coming to this earth that would need me to be their mother, and I am grateful that I have been able to fulfill my divine feminine destiny.

Chapter 3

THE GIFT OF MIRACLES

It is truly amazing when heaven touches us in ways that can only be called miracles. Many times we don't recognize the miracles in our lives as they occur. We see them later, when we look back with perfect hindsight and notice what has happened. But occasionally we do it right—we are fully aware, and we are entirely grateful.

In the October 2007 general conference, President Henry B. Eyring counseled us to look for God's hand in our lives and to record those moments in a journal (see "'O Remember, Remember,'" *Ensign*, November 2007, 66–69). I choose to call these experiences miracles.

How do we go about calling down the powers of heaven? First and foremost, we must have faith and let God take over. We must have the strength and the faith to allow God to fulfill His plan for our life.

EXPECTING A MIRACLE

The first stumbling block we hit is the desire to tell Heavenly Father just exactly what we expect for our miracle.

In a file where I keep thoughts and poems, I came across an old greeting card that communicated to me just how my relationship with God should be. It read:

Then I heard His footsteps along the path I trod
And He softly whispered to me, "My child, let go . . . Let God"

I have learned this lesson in my own life over and over again.

A few years ago, Hal's daughter, Noël, was diagnosed with ovarian cancer. Noël was a wonderful woman and had loved me from the beginning of my relationship with her father. Her illness was such a sad time. Hal prayed such humble prayers in her behalf. When they told us about her illness, Hal got down on his knees.

When I asked him what he had asked for, he said, "Well, I told Heavenly Father, you either have to give her a miracle of healing, or you have to carry her in your arms across the veil so she won't be afraid."

Noël's husband gave up his job and career to care for her full time in a tiny apartment next to the cancer institute. They tried every possible treatment to heal her. When we visited her, Noël was so happy just because she had a beautiful tree to look at outside of her bedroom window. Her attitude could not have been better, but it was very difficult for the rest of us to deal with the effects of the cancer on her.

On March 6, 1992, at about three in the morning, we received the dreaded call that she had passed away. I was scheduled to give a talk the next day, and I had to catch an early flight. I told Hal I would stay home with him, but he always felt I could do more good on my speaking assignments, so he insisted that I go.

When I returned home, Hal was just beaming with contentment. I was surprised and asked him, "Are you feeling okay about everything?"

He said, "I'm going to tell you what happened. After you left, I knelt down by the bed where I had prayed to Heavenly Father for a miracle. I said, 'Okay, I want to know. You didn't heal her, so did you carry her across the veil?'" Hal then told me that he had felt Noël's presence in the room, and then he felt as though he heard her say, "Daddy, I am gloriously happy."

Hal said, "I didn't see her, but I recognized her voice. Noël is the only one that would have said, 'gloriously happy.'" He knew that his daughter was okay. She had received her miracle.

ELEVEN YEARS OF MIRACLES

Just a month after Noël's death, Hal and I went to Boulder, Colorado, to visit our granddaughter, Kristina, who was attending the university there. After a nice dinner together, we returned to the hotel. At about four in the morning Hal awakened with a high fever. The paramedics rushed him to the hospital. His heart began racing, and he was rushed to intensive care.

I remember sitting on the floor with a telephone book and calling our friends, Elder Robert and Sister Helen Wells, asking them to help me find someone to give Hal a blessing. While I was on the phone, I heard over the intercom the words, "Emergency to ICU." In that instant I knew it was because of Hal. I hung up and rushed to ICU. For the first time, they wouldn't let me in. I knew the worst was happening.

I grabbed Kristina and asked, "Do you have faith?" And together we prayed. I then said the hardest words I've ever said in my life: "Nevertheless, not my will, but Thine be done." At that moment, I gave my husband to the Lord's care. Just then they called me into the ICU. They said they were going to use a new drug to slow Hal's racing heart rate.

Just a few minutes later, the phone rang, and the nurse said, "Are you Sister Jones?" I was puzzled. Why did she call me Sister Jones?

I was handed the phone, and the man on the other end said, "Sister Jones, I'm Bishop Larsen. I can give your husband a blessing."

I said, "Did you come at the request of Elder Wells?"

The bishop said, "No, I was walking down the hall here at the hospital, and your granddaughter ran into the hall and asked, 'Are you a Mormon bishop?'

"I said, 'Yes, I am.'

"She said, 'My grandpa needs you!'"

Hal's miracle began to unfold. He received a priesthood blessing, and his heart immediately improved. We flew on an air ambulance to our home and down from high altitude. He had taken a big step backward physically, but he was still with us and ready to do the things necessary to continue living a righteous life.

Hal's doctors warned him not to travel to a high altitude again, but Gretchen, a former Miss USA I had worked with and a dear friend, had joined the Church and was getting married in the Salt Lake Temple. Because her parents were not members, she needed us to act as her mother and father in the sealing room. Hal, looking as white as a sheet, took the enormous risk and once again flew to a high-altitude destination and stood in for her father on her special day.

Only a few days after returning home, our son, John, called in severe depression. The suicide death of his natural father (my first husband) had been a disastrous event when he was a young child. I had always been grateful that I had married Hal and that he had raised John as his own son. John had served a mission in Argentina, but his temple marriage had ended in divorce. He was depressed, and the disastrous thought struck me, "Could he possibly follow in the footsteps of his biological father?" My stomach churned at the thought of losing a son. What could I do? I kept in close contact, but I had to let go and let God. It took some time, but a miracle in John's life was developing.

In the meantime, Hal was scheduled for emergency open heart surgery. I had been praying constantly that the Lord would be there to guide the hands of the surgeon, and Hal had heard my prayers. The next morning as they were wheeling him into the operating room, I said, "Don't forget who will be with you." Hal said, rather loudly, "Jesus Christ."

Things did not go entirely smoothly. There had been some unexpected heavy bleeding, and the surgery went several hours longer than predicted. I found a note Hal had written and placed on top of his wallet. It said, "I'll go where you want me to go, dear Lord." At that moment, I knew that Hal was prepared and willing to submit to the will of the Lord, but I was not. I was humbled by this realization.

Our surgeon, Dr. Walji, knew that we were LDS. The next morning, he saw me in the cafeteria and asked me to sit with him. I had always felt that he was a very spiritual man, and I felt the presence of the Spirit as he told me of his experience in the operating room with Hal. He told me that Hal was a high-risk patient for this type of operation. The chances for complications were especially high after the bypasses were completed and the heart needed to be restarted with an electrical shock. At this point, there was a great risk of stroke or other complications. But at the moment when he needed to give the heart a shock, Hal's heart started beating on its own. Quietly, Dr. Walji said simply, "I am only a mechanic. God is in charge."

One night, after I had left the hospital, I called from home to check on him. His heart was in atrial fibrillation, a dangerous situation for him.

When I knelt to pray, I saw that the clock read 11:02. I asked that the Lord intervene. I rose and sat on the bed. The clock read 11:11. I called the cardiac care unit, and the nurse answered my query by saying, "Good news. Your husband's heart just converted back to normal rhythm eight minutes ago." It was exactly the time I had asked for the Lord's help. Yet another miracle.

Now, what was left to go wrong? Well, our daughter, Wendy, was serving a mission in Honduras. The mission president had called to say that the missionaries were on a terrorist hit list. The mission would be evacuated. Wendy would be flying home within twenty-four hours. The constant worry during that entire dangerous time was overwhelming. She finally did return safely home.

By fall of that year, Hal was recovering. John had found a wonderful girl and was in love. Wendy was home safely from Honduras. Then I fell apart. I suffer from migraines, and at this time was beginning my eleventh straight day of uninterrupted pain. I kept begging Heavenly Father to help me. Finally, I couldn't even think anymore. I fell to my knees to pray, but the words wouldn't come. The tears streamed down my cheeks. It was then that I heard the still, small voice say, "Go to the temple." I heard that instruction two additional times because I was hesitant. It would take an hour to get there. I would have to get dressed up to go. My head was throbbing. My vision was blurred. I didn't know if I could make it through a two-hour session.

I started getting dressed. I got in my car and drove rather blindly through the traffic. This was insane! The temple was crowded. It was a Saturday, and there were brides and wedding parties everywhere. I got dressed and went to sit in the chapel until the session was ready. I could feel my headache getting worse. I slipped out to take some more medicine. I returned to the chapel. I opened the scriptures to Doctrine and Covenants 101:16 and read: "Be still and know that I am God." I was overwhelmed with His Spirit. I began to cry. The more I read, the more I cried. It was not what I was reading, but it was the Spirit bearing witness to me that He wanted me to come because He loved me. "Come unto me, all ye that labour and are heavy laden, and I will give you rest" (Matthew 11:28). That's what I needed so badly. I had to be in a place such as the temple where His Spirit could speak to me and I would listen. The Lord seemed to say to me, "Barbara, why haven't you come to me? You have tried to take on all of these cares all by yourself. You can't do it."

In that instant, I realized that this was why I was breaking down. I needed to have faith to listen to the Spirit. I had been guided to the temple. I cried in the chapel for forty minutes. As I went into the session, I received another testimony of the hereafter. I knew that Noël and I would one day hold hands and together happily see all of the beautiful places of the world together.

At the completion of the session, as I went through the veil, I felt the Lord's Spirit with me in the celestial room. It seemed we communicated for some time. I remember most that I needed to open myself to His Spirit and really listen. In other words, I needed to quit trying to do everything my way and let go and let God.

The stresses of life had been more than I alone could bear, but with Him it would be easier. He indicated that my family would be fine and that I was doing the work He wanted me to do. He loves me, but I couldn't forget to come unto Him.

I felt such a sense of relief as I left the temple. My headache was gone, and my spirit was filled to overflowing. I had heeded the promptings of the Spirit, and my Heavenly Father had helped me. And even though I would have struggles and trials, I was headed in the right direction. I had finally let go and let God. I could continue to expect miracles.

THE GREATEST MIRACLE

The greatest miracle of my life would not happen for another decade. Hal suffered with heart problems for thirteen years. He believed emphatically that Heavenly Father had carried him all those years. As he got harder of hearing, he would walk through the house saying loudly, "Well, Heavenly Father, thanks for carrying me. I know I'm getting a little heavier each day. I'm ready to go whenever you are."

Hal passed away at the age of eighty-six on March 6, 2003, eleven years to the day after Noël passed away. I was away from home on a speaking assignment in Salt Lake City. Before I left, we uncharacteristically cried together. I had begged the Lord for years to please allow me to be with him at that time. But it was not to be. Another type of miracle awaited me.

I had been asked to bear my testimony to the cast of a theatre production, "The Savior of the World," a wonderful musical production put on in the Conference Center in Salt Lake City and dedicated to the life of the Savior. I went to their rehearsal with a friend, who said, "The cast is in here. We'll just go and sit in the back until they're ready for you to speak."

As my friend opened the door, I heard the most celestial voices. The entire cast of almost one hundred was dressed in white robes like angels, singing. At that moment, I had the revelation that this is what Hal would experience as he passed through the veil. I started to cry. I knew then that I was being prepared for what was about to happen.

That night I called Hal and told him of my experience with the angels and that they would be singing to him when he crossed the veil. Hal said,

Until we meet again . . .

"Well, I'm not sure exactly what will happen, but I know it's going to be good." The next evening I received a phone call telling me that my husband had just passed away. He had been feeling fine and was walking through the house for a little exercise and had just lain down to rest for a moment. Suddenly, I was grateful that Heavenly Father had prepared me, and I knew for sure that Hal had heard the angels singing. I was reminded of this line from Shakespeare's *Hamlet:* "Good night sweet prince: And flights of angels sing thee to thy rest!" (V, ii).

When my daughter, Wendy, flew back to San Francisco with me that night, my four-year-old granddaughter, Noël, named for her aunt, saw her mother and me crying. Not knowing what to do, she stood and started singing at the top of her lungs, "The sun will come out tomorrow, bet your bottom dollar that tomorrow there'll be sun . . ." We had to smile. In fact, the entire plane was smiling. She sang the entire song. You can smile through your tears at times like these, when God gives us "beauty for ashes, the oil of joy for mourning, [and] the garment of praise for the spirit of heaviness . . ." (Isaiah 61:3).

But what about my miracle? I had asked for only one small miracle, to be there when he passed away. But the Lord says, "For my thoughts are not your thoughts, neither are your ways my ways, saith the Lord.

"For as the heavens are higher than the earth, so are my ways higher than your ways, and my thoughts than your thoughts" (Isaiah 55:8–9).

Heavenly Father was letting me know that I had to let go and let Him direct my life. He knew what was best.

After the viewing, I placed Hal's temple recommend and our photograph together in his hands. The words of Michael McLean's song "Together Forever Someday" kept going through my mind:

And for all this love thank the Lord above

Who showed us the way

That we can be together forever someday.

(Used with permission by Deseret Book /
Shadow Mountain Music)

The Atonement has now taken on new meaning in my life. My eyes have been opened to eternal life and joy. Because of the Lord's covenant, Hal and I can be together someday, and that is the real miracle! Yes, Heavenly Father was right when He said, "I am a God of miracles" (2 Nephi 27:23).

JoAnn's Story

It was 11 PM as I drove to the dorms at BYU–Hawaii on a very hot August night. I was exhausted! I had with me a woman from Holland named JoAnn Sparks, whom I had just met and offered to drive back to

JoAnn before coming to America

JoAnn today, Stake Relief Society President

her room. As she thanked me for the ride, she said in a sweet voice, "Do you have time for me to tell you my story?" I breathed deeply, "Of course I do." Then I literally sat spellbound for more than an hour. I cried when she told me her story, an example of God's miraculous intervention. I share it here with her permission.

I was born and raised in Holland just as World War II was starting. I do remember being hungry many nights because my dad was in a work camp in Germany and my mother had been in a bike accident and couldn't take care of us.

I remember when the war ended and how happy everyone was. That is vivid in my memory. In many ways, our life returned to normal, but we didn't have a happy childhood.

When I was eighteen, my sister and my brother-in-law invited me to come and visit their home because they were going to have the Mormon missionaries over. I was impressed. The missionaries and the discussions we had gave me peace and comfort. All three of us joined the Church.

As time went on, I looked around at our branch. There were maybe fifteen people there, ranging in age from eight to eighty. I knew that there was no chance I would meet an eternal companion there or marry in the temple. I told my parents that I wanted to leave and go to America. My dad wanted me to stay until I was twenty-one. I turned twenty-one on June 15th, and on June 17th I was on the boat to America.

I needed a sponsor. I had talked to an American missionary serving in Holland. He wrote to his mother, and they said that I could come and stay with them for a while. The boat trip took ten days, and it was three days and two nights on the train to cross the country to Utah. I came to the town of Ogden, and I remember very well how impressed I was. I did not speak the language, and I didn't know anyone, so I had some real challenges awaiting me.

I stayed with my missionary family while I was arranging for a job as a nanny. I was told that at my job I would have my own room with my own television and furniture. I could not yet communicate with the children or the parents.

My friend took me to the home. She asked the parents, "Shall I take her suitcase to her room?" because she wanted to see where I would be staying. They refused. We didn't know it at the time, but the family was going through some tough situations.

I learned quickly why the couple didn't want my friend to see my room. The house was in complete disarray. When the family took me to my room, there was no chair, only a baby bed filled with clothes that needed to be ironed. I started to turn down the bed, but someone had wet the mattress several times, and the bedding reeked of urine. I thought I would just sit on the floor, but it was too dirty. I thought I'd hang my clothes in the closet, but when I opened it, cockroaches came streaming out. So, I just stood there all night, holding my suitcase off the floor and crying.

The next day, the parents left for work. I was shown the refrigerator, which was filthy, and a sink filled with dirty dishes. The children were so mean to me. They would make fun because I couldn't speak the language, and they were extremely disrespectful to both their parents and me. I persuaded the children to play outside. I cleaned all day and kept busy because I was so sleepy. I washed the walls, but I didn't eat. Again I stood through the night. I prayed, "Heavenly Father, if I've made a mistake, please provide a way for me to go home." I soon found that the Lord had already provided help through a wonderful woman.

When I had first arrived, I met another missionary who had served in Holland. He had just married, and he wanted me to come to dinner and meet his wife. On the day I started my nanny job, I went to their home. His mother came by on her way home from work to meet me and visit for a while. She took me aside and said that if I ever needed any help, I was to call her. She gave me her name and phone number. And the most remarkable thing of all was that she could understand Dutch. It was wonderful to be able to communicate with someone.

I called her after the second day at my job. She said that she would take me to her home. She couldn't pick me up that night, but she would come first thing the next morning. I didn't know what to tell the family. I was young and scared. She came at 6 AM, and I was ready. I don't really know what was said to the family, but from that day on, this woman took over as if she were my mother. She had never had a daughter, and she treated me like her own. She made appointments for me. She had a wonderful room ready for me and fed me well.

Through a member of the bishopric, I got a job at a nice seafood restaurant. I still could not speak English, and my co-workers and I communicated by sign language. I will always remember one special day at work. As I looked out the window, a limousine with a chauffer and two older people stopped in front. One of my co-workers tried to ask me if I knew who it was. I watched as the older man walked around to let his wife out. I simply did not recognize them. I had always seen younger pictures of this gentleman, and I did not know who it was. Finally, she said that it was President David O. McKay.

My co-worker said that once they got settled, she would introduce me to him. She said that he came there often and that it was his favorite restaurant. He often came before the restaurant opened so that they could eat in peace. When President McKay arrived, they told him that there was a girl from Holland who worked there and who was LDS, but she didn't speak English. President McKay asked to meet me.

When I got to the table, President McKay stood up. My co-worker introduced me to him and said, "President McKay, this is JoAnn from Holland. She is a convert to the Church." He was very kind to me, and he invited me to sit down with him and his wife. He talked to me for quite a few minutes, but I did not understand him. The only thing I could think was, "No one will believe me that I am sitting here talking to a prophet."

He was so friendly and sweet, but I really did not know what he was saying. I had this fear that I had bothered him too long. Finally I decided to stand up. I have often wondered if it was in the middle of a sentence or if he thought I was being rude. As I stood, he also stood up. He took my hand and said, "Sister JoAnn, I have a message for you. It is the Lord's will that you came to this country. You have an important mission here to fulfill." The amazing thing was that I understood every word he said because he was speaking to me in perfect Dutch!

The minute he finished his message to me from Heavenly Father, I heard him in English again. And I could no longer understand a single word he was saying. I had heard about the gift of tongues, and I know that particular message was a miracle. After that day, I never felt I was a foreigner again.

I then returned to my work. I've often wondered why something that special would happen to me. I only know that I was grateful for the tremendous experience.

After that day, I started learning English very rapidly and well. I just started picking it up. I suddenly knew how to spell words. I would see the words in my mind, spelled out like they were on a sign. I felt like the Lord was taking me by the hand. I soon became a bookkeeper and met my future husband, who was a neighbor; I married the boy next door. We were married three months later in the Logan Utah Temple. We were blessed with three wonderful children, and everything went well from the day that I met David O. McKay. I knew I belonged in this country, and I knew that it was Heavenly Father's will. I know that He directed my life.

I know with all my heart that the gospel is true, that our Heavenly Father loves us and that He truly is aware of each one of us personally. It was a happy day for me when my son fulfilled a mission to pay back the debt that I owed our Heavenly Father for bringing the gospel into my life. I think I have held every position in the Church that a woman can hold.

Heavenly Father knows us, He is only a prayer away, He can bless us with miracles.

Chapter 4

THE GIFT OF HUMOR

To start a chapter on humor, I must share one of the funniest stories I know. This is a true story that happened to a dear friend, Wanda Swenson.

Wanda's husband was a distributor for Wrigley's Spearmint gum. Each week, after filling all his orders, he would call the company and they would send a delivery person to his home to replenish his supply. The deliveryman knew exactly where to leave the cases in Brother Swenson's garage.

One particularly hectic morning, after the children had left for school and Wanda had fed the baby, she decided that she would throw in a quick load of laundry before starting her day. Still in her nightgown, holding the baby in one arm, she grabbed the laundry basket and headed for the washing machine in the corner of garage. The first thing she spotted on the garage floor was her son's football helmet. She put the laundry basket down, threw the clothes in the washer, picked up the helmet, and lacking another hand to carry it, plopped it on to her head. Then the baby spat up all of the recently eaten rice cereal on Wanda's nightgown. Spit up was everywhere and had soaked through to the skin. In desperation, she put the baby under one arm horizontally, stripped down to nothing, and threw the soiled clothing into the washing machine. Get the picture!

At that very moment, the garage door started to open. It was the delivery man! She decided to "freeze!" Maybe he would not notice. He took two big cases out of his trunk and carried them to the designated spot. He repeated this several times without so much as a glance in her direction. As the trunk was emptied and he was leaving, he said, "Say lady, I sure hope your team wins."

I hope that you are laughing aloud at this moment or even just smiling. Laughter is so important; it makes life more fun.

Elder Henry B. Eyring said, "Keep your eyes open for humor in the present. The people I know who are good for the long haul all seem to smile easily. . . . The incongruities of giving more than you seem to get guarantee the chance to smile. I hope you will. All it will take is to keep your eyes open. And I think it's a key to endurance" (*Because He First Loved Us,* 104, 106).

President Thomas S. Monson spoke of the privilege it was to serve for many years with President Spencer W. Kimball when he was chairman of the Missionary Executive Council: "Those never-to-be-forgotten missionary assignment meetings were filled with inspiration and occasionally interspersed with humor. Well do I remember the recommendation form of one prospective missionary on which the bishop had written: 'This young man is very close to his mother. She wonders if he might be assigned to a mission close to home in California so that she can visit him on occasion and telephone him weekly.' As I read aloud this comment, I awaited from President Kimball the pronouncement of a designated assignment. I noticed a twinkle in his eye and a sweet smile across his lips as he said, without additional comment, 'Assign him to the South Africa Johannesburg Mission'" (*Be Your Best Self,* 59–60).

WE BECOME WHAT WE FEEL

A little girl looked at her mom and said, "Mommy, are you happy?"
The mother replied, "Of course I'm happy."
Her daughter said, "Well, why don't you ever tell your face?"
This is really more true than funny. As they say, "Smile and the whole world smiles with you! Cry and you cry alone."

I think Heavenly Father is mindful of all the things we need in life, even humor. But I think that we as women can sometimes forget what it's like to smile or laugh.

To truly change our lives, we need to understand that how we think and feel, how we react to the things that happen to us, will dictate the course of our lives. John Milton wrote, "The mind is its own place, and in itself/ can make a Heav'n of Hell, a Hell of Heav'n" (*Paradise Lost,* book 1, lines 254–55).

Scientific research has long reported that laughing releases potent endorphins in our bodies, providing an "inner upper." I can testify that this research is absolutely correct. During the last year of my husband Hal's life, I had to call the paramedics five times. I came to know the EMTs, and they were used to me and the fact that in stressful times I tended to joke around. That same year, I also had a total hip replacement, and I didn't know the limits of what I could and couldn't do during my recovery. One day, while Hal was in the hospital, I was scheduled to do a talk. I was throwing stuff in my suitcase and decided I had time for a short workout. I was doing some stretches, and my new hip popped right out of the socket. I was in pain! I couldn't stand up, so I pulled myself over to the desk, pulled down the phone, and called 911.

When the paramedics came to my house, they could see me on the floor through the window. The doors were locked, and I couldn't get to them. At first, they thought I was kidding around and started laughing at me. I was motioning for help, and they were looking at me through the window and waving.

I yelled to them, "I have dislocated my new hip." Now, my hip pain had become unbearable.

They finally got the message and broke a window. There I was, lying on the floor in my Steve Young number eight football jersey and old sweatpants. They got the stretcher out just like the ones they use to take the football players off the field. Every movement was excruciating.

I couldn't help myself. I could see the humor in this. So, I partially sat up and started waving at the non-existent crowd, just like Steve Young would have done. The paramedics started laughing so hard they almost dropped me. We laughed all the way to the hospital. And you know what? I had much less pain.

Once I arrived at the hospital and was left alone, the pain returned and was very intense. It proved to me that humor and laughter can control pain by distracting attention, reducing tension, and increasing production of endorphins, the body's natural painkillers. Indeed, laughter really is the best medicine.

A PRESCRIPTION FOR HUMOR

To get your own dose of this powerful medicine, you must first understand that different things make different people laugh. You actually have to learn which style of humor tickles you the most. How? Practice telling jokes, spend an hour browsing the news for funny headlines, laugh at yourself, begin using humor to defuse stress. Soon, you'll find a handful of things that instantly make the corners of your mouth turn up.

After I gave a fireside about the effects of humor in relationships, I received an e-mail from one of the husbands in the audience. He wrote:

"After we returned home from your fireside, Jane and I went to our room. I asked her if she liked the fireside, and 40 minutes later, she asked me what I thought about it. Of course my answer was, 'It was great.' She laughed, and we set some goals to implement humor into our lives.

"The next morning, Sunday, Jane and I were in bed asleep. John and Alan were up. John got the cereal off the top of the fridge to make breakfast. He set the box on the burner and accidentally turned it on to high. He then went to see if Alan wanted cereal, too. Returning to the kitchen, he found the smoke detector going off and a fire with billowing smoke coming from the stove. He started to panic and came in our room to wake us up. Jane went flying off the bed like Super Mom, and I was right on her heels.

"At the kitchen doorway we surveyed the scene and could see exactly what had happened. The boys were huddled in the corner crying. They knew they must be in trouble. I looked at Jane and said, 'Remember the fireside? Let's try it! Let's try to handle this with humor.' She smiled. We ran first to put out the fire. Then, rather than yelling and getting upset at the boys, which is how we would have normally responded, we smiled and high-fived them both. We praised John for acting fast in getting us involved. Because of him, our house did not burn down, and he was a hero. Both boys were shocked at our actions but by now were smiling through their tears. We started airing out the house and while cleaning up, Jane made cereal to give to the boys and said, 'Boys, how would you like your cereal, hot or cold?' I gave Jane a hug and told her she was incredible. We then talked about how blessed we had been to be able to maintain our composure and make lemonade from lemons. Had it not been for your fireside, we are convinced that our reaction would have had long-term disastrous results. As a result, this experience has become a testimony builder to the power and truthfulness of the things taught to us, as well as the Lord's influence in our lives."

Humor is a skill. For some people, it doesn't come naturally at first. But you can learn. You can learn how to find positive and life-affirming humor in many situations.

Author, humorist, and member of the American Medical Association, Loretta LaRoche, writes that nearly 75 percent of the things we say each day are negative. From morning to night, we complain and talk about negative things: "It's raining outside."

"My back is just killing me."

"I'm so bloated."

"I have a horrible headache."

"Did you know that I just had my hip replaced?"

"I'm so tired. I just never get enough sleep."

Watch yourself! People don't want to listen to someone who is always down. LaRoche writes about her Italian family and her grandmother, who was really into suffering. She wore black just in case someone died. In contrast, her grandfather, who had only one arm, was an eternal optimist and laughed about everything.

LaRoche points out that children laugh four hundred times a day. Adults laugh about fifteen times. Learn from the children. One day, when LaRoche went to visit her little three-year-old granddaughter, she found her standing stark naked in front of a mirror wearing her mother's high heels and applauding herself. When was the last time you did that? Or anything remotely close to expressing feelings of self-approval?

It's easy to increase your ability to laugh. You simply need to look for reasons to laugh. And there really are no rules for humor except to avoid causing hurt to others. If you're like me, you won't have to look very far to find something to laugh about it. Let me share a few personal stories.

All Wet. One night I was all dressed up and ready to go to a dinner party with some friends. I had put an orchid corsage in our fishpond, and I went to retrieve it. The orchid had floated to the other side of the water-fall, so I put my foot on a rock to take a step. The rock tipped, and I fell flat in the fishpond. There I was with fish poop all over me and little gold-fish swimming back and forth over my body wondering what was going on. My friends didn't know whether to laugh or cry. I burst out laughing, and they joined me. Of course, they had to wait for me to take a shower and get everything out of my hair before we could leave. But it was hilarious.

The Snow Queen. When I was younger, I was dancing the role of Snow Queen in *The Nutcracker* during the scene where the King and Queen in the Land of Snow have the pas de deux. I came out on my part-ner's shoulder, gliding across the front of the stage, my arms gracefully moving from side to side. The audience broke up laughing. I couldn't believe it. And I couldn't imagine why they were laugh-ing. Did I have toilet paper attached? Was it actually me? Then, out of the corner of my eye, I saw the problem. Our ballet director's white poodle was prancing along behind us. It was my big

Barbara as the Snow Queen in the Nutcracker

opportunity, and I was upstaged by a poodle. Thirty years later, the scene is even more funny. Remember, crisis + time = humor.

A Nest of Swarming Bees? Christy wasn't LDS, but she attended church with my husband and me the first Sunday of the month. It was fast and testimony meeting. I had gone to the stand to bear my testimony and was waiting my turn. I had a perfect view of her face as she listened to another sister bear her testimony. The sister began, "I just want my Beehives to know how much I love them."

I looked at Christy, and she had a shocked look on her face. Beehives?

The lady went on. "Yesterday I loaded my Beehives into my van, and I took them to the beach."

Christy's eyes got bigger!

"When we got to the beach, I opened the door, and they went everywhere. It was hard to gather them up and get them back into the van. They talked all the way home. I just want my Beehives to know how much I love them."

By this time, Christy's eyes were the size of saucers. As the lady walked down from the stand, Christy leaned over to one of the brethren next to her and, with an incredulous voice, asked, "Why did she take her beehives to the beach?"

The man looked back at her and said, "I guess that's where they wanted to go."

Humor is all around us. It's part of our lives, and looking for it can keep us happy and healthy.

Use Close Personal Friends

I have a wonderful sidekick (she's very close to me) named Melweena. She has to wear glasses, so she chooses to wear the most outrageous, highly decorated ones she can find. She also has false teeth. Melweena just adores telling jokes, and sometimes she elbows me out of the way at the oddest times. I just can't completely control her; but she helps me find the humor in my life.

Here are some of Melweena's favorite thoughts on women. Some of these you have heard before, and they are certainly corny, but as my friend Brad Wilcox says, "They may be corny, but people eat corn."

Melweena Dweeb, my sidekick and alter ego

- You know, age is just a number . . . and mine's unlisted. ☺
- Now, I don't repeat gossip . . . so listen carefully. ☺
- My mind not only wanders . . . sometimes it leaves completely. ☺
- Like the other day . . . I went to the top of the stairs, and I forgot what I went for. Then I was sitting in a chair and started to get up but forgot what I was getting up for. But I'm sure I'm not losing my mind, knock on wood . . . Oh, excuse me, there's someone at the door. ☺
- The nice part about living in a small town is that when you don't know what you're doing . . . someone else does. ☺
- Sometimes I think I understand everything . . . then I regain consciousness. ☺
- That's why insanity is my only means of relaxation. ☺

- Do you know why women over fifty don't have babies? . . . Because they would put them down and forget where they left them. ☺
- Did you hear about the lady who got her Valium mixed up with her birth control pills? She had fourteen children, and she didn't even care! ☺
- My favorite women's joke is: Who puts the leaves on the trees in the springtime? The Re-leaf Society. ☺

Look for humor in your life. Laugh long and loud. It's the best way. Melweena gets to say and do a lot of things that I could never get away with. I just put on a pair of her glasses, insert her teeth, and there she is. She is such a scream. She's got a joke for every occasion, and best of all, she can get my family laughing.

Acquire Props. If you're looking for ways to add humor to your life, I suggest getting some props. Nothing works quite so well as a magic wand. It's nice to have a crown to go with it, but the real necessity is the magic wand. Take a few warm-up swings, then go into your teenage daughter's bedroom and announce, "I'm the queen of this house."

You'll have her attention. Then say, "I can't believe your room is such a mess. The queen requests that you clean it."

Before she can ask you where you got the crown, say, "Never mind, I'm the queen of this house. Just for today, I'm going to help you clean your room."

Then pitch in and make cleaning the room a lot of fun. Laugh together. It will make a huge difference.

Even when you need to be serious, humor can work. One lady I know bought a Darth Vader mask. Now, instead of telling her family, "Just do it because I said so," she puts on the mask and says, "You will obey." Her kids love it, and they know she means it.

Just try a few things and see what works. Wear a red foam nose to dinner and see where the discussion goes after you answer the "why" questions. It will definitely be memorable—and fun.

Keep a Humor Notebook. One of the best suggestions I've ever heard is to keep a humor notebook. It really works. A few years ago, my husband and I started keeping little humorous items. I kept mine in a notebook, and he had a little place in his wallet where he kept jokes.

I suggest you do the same. Let your imagination run wild. Use your scrapbooking skills if you would like, but get your family together and make a notebook or folder for each member of the family. Have each person gather jokes, cartoons, or just write about something funny that happened. Just think how the grumpy attitudes of teens will change if they are keeping an eye out for something funny. Or think how you will face the annoyances of life when you're mentally writing all about it in your

Madison and her cat, Beauty-Lila.
A "Kodak moment" for my humor first aid kit.

humor notebook. It can't help but make you smile. And when you start smiling, good things happen.

Your notebook can serve as a humor first-aid kit. I have the cutest picture of my granddaughter Madison and her cat drinking milk off the floor. She poured a half gallon of milk on the floor because she was pretending to be a kitty. All I have to do is look at it to make me smile.

Start a collection of comic videos you can watch. Doctors at leading medical centers are continuing to study the advantageous effects of laughter and how it can make scientifically measurable improvements. It is hard to argue with medical science, but, repeatedly, humor proves to be awfully powerful and positive medicine.

When you laugh, you feel renewed and revitalized. Humor is so closely connected to joy. In addition, when joy overwhelms us, it feels like the sun is coming out. The darkness of your problems is chased into the corners, and you can bask for a moment in light and gladness.

The book of Psalms was written as prayers of thanksgiving to God. Laughter is part of that praise. "Then was our mouth filled with laughter, and our tongue with singing" (Psalm 126:2).

My parents adopted my little sister Paula when I was ten and Paula was three. Paula had lots of friends in school. She was popular, but she didn't care about grades. When Paula finished high school, she "ran away" and joined the circus!

Paula's life took a turn at age thirty-five. My favorite statement about my sister is that she went from fire-spitter to Ph.D. Her story is a perfect example of getting through life using the gift of humor. I reprint her story here, with her permission.

THE PAULA DUVANDER STORY

Hi, I'm Paula, and I recently read a new book about specific life paths. Amazingly, the path that supposedly fit my life perfectly was the one I took. The book told me, "When Shakespeare wrote, 'All the world is a stage,' he was talking about you." The book described people like me as comediennes, actors, and singers, as well as natural counselors, who are able to see the potential in others. "People love to be around you," the book explained, "because you are great company. You use your fine sense of humor to get you through the bad days. Laughter is what saves you."

With the previous paragraph in mind, I would like to share with you my story. I was adopted by wonderful parents and raised in a border town in Texas. I was somewhat tomboyish and especially loved pretending to be a cowgirl. I was so captivated by this lifestyle that often I became a cowgirl named Stoney Sunset. (As you can see, my "life path" of being a performer was beginning.)

Now, Stoney Sunset had an older sister who was the exact opposite. Her prissy sister, Barbara, always dressed up, was on the honor roll, and was always the teacher's pet. Stoney hated to dress up. She preferred jeans to skirts any day! She didn't make the greatest grades in school but enjoyed the social aspect. Stoney was a cheerleader and also performed on television, singing and dancing with a local high school group known as the "Group and D.K." She took ballet classes and even performed in a melodrama theatre. Three weeks after graduating from high school, Stoney, now known as Paula, got into a Volkswagen Bug and moved across the United States.

I wanted to be independent and follow my sister, Barbara, who was doing something glamorous as a professional ballet dancer. I was ready to discover for myself that "all the world is a stage." However, my goals were sketchy. I had no skills, so I went to work as a telephone operator.

It was then that I met Greg, and we were married. We were both very young and didn't have a lot in common. We parted ways after seven years. I found an apartment and placed my mattress on the floor. I had a little TV, a couch, and was ready for a new start. The problem was the balance in my checkbook—12 cents.

Hurray! I got a job working in the box office and performing in the children's theatre in Atlanta, Georgia. This was something that had been in my dreams for some time. I took acting classes and was able to be with "theatre folks." That is where I learned to juggle. What fun!

Next, I landed a job working for the famous brother-sister team of Sid and Marty Krofft, the creators of television character H.R. Pufnstuf. We worked in an enormous indoor amusement park similar to Disneyland but with life-sized puppet cartoon characters, mimes, jugglers, clowns, and so on.

Out of the blue, my friends Andy and Nancy called one night and asked if I wanted to come and stay at their house in California. I was only twenty-five and still firmly believed all the world was my stage, so I was off to California! I lived in their tiny storage shed in the backyard. There was exactly room enough for a single mattress. There was no heat and only my electric blanket for warmth. It was freezing!

One night Nancy and I went to visit Barbara and Hal who now lived only an hour away. I had promised Hal that I would spit fire for him. We went outside. I filled my mouth with kerosene and proceeded to "spit" the kerosene through my front teeth as Nancy put the flame to it. Hal loved telling people, "I have a sister-in-law who can really spit fire!" Then he would laugh and laugh.

Later I was off to the world-famous Dell'Arte School of Mime and Comedy, where people came from all over the world to gain the skills to work for Barnum and Bailey, Ringling Brothers, Hollywood films, and Disneyland. It was there I learned to perfect my fire-spitting skills and other "useful" skills, such as walking the tight rope. After graduation I was hired for a one-year tour of the United States with the Kit and Kaboodle mime troupe. We were five people in a van with everything we owned. The traveling was one-night stands, sleeping on the floor, and the pay was lousy. All that had glittered turned out not to be gold!

Now my life took a drastic turn. I went to work for a residential treatment center that helped severely disturbed children. It was there I met my next husband, Richard, and did the job of counseling for which I had a talent but no education. I worked there for a number of years. I was thirty-five years old when I left the treatment center and took my first class in arithmetic at a junior college. Then I took another class and another class and . . . I received my baccalaureate at age thirty-eight. I got my master's degree at forty-one while working full-time. I started building my practice as a marriage and family therapist. I then went back and got my doctorate degree at age forty-eight. Persistence pays off!

During my college years I used my background from comedy school and entertaining to tie in laughter and humor with therapy. I did research on humor and the immune system. I worked extensively with children in what is known as "play therapy."

In retrospect, I've learned some real life skills, and one of those is that looking at the lighter side of life gives us balance. Laughter and looking for humor, those lighter elements, remind us of what was good about a bad situation.

As an example, I remember going to visit my mom during the last few years of her life when she was in a nursing home suffering with Alzheimer's. Those visits were pretty sad.

I can remember one visit when a psychiatrist had been called in to give our family a definite diagnosis. He asked her different questions to which she mostly responded with accuracy. However, he kept repeating the question, "Mrs. Harrell, what year is it?"

From the very beginning of his visit, she continued to answer this question with the same incorrect year. After he left, she said, "Well, I'll never know how he got to be a doctor, he doesn't even know what year it is!"

Another time when I flew in for a visit, I decided to wear an outfit with cheerful colors that would brighten her day. I chose a lemon-yellow scarf, a bright pink shirt, and a pair of purple pants. When I walked into the room, she said to me, "Those colors make you look big!"

I said, "Well, I am big."

She responded, "Well, that explains it!" Oh, have I laughed thinking about that day.

While working as a therapist and going through life, my husband, Richard, became very ill. He was diagnosed with a cancerous brain tumor. It was terminal, and he was given six months to live. I would always counsel my clients that when you are feeling morose, humor is a choice that makes things lighter and more bearable.

During Richard's illness, his unusual actions were due to the effects of the tumor on his brain. One night I heard him in the den laughing aloud. When I went to check on him, he was watching TV. I asked him what was so funny, and he proceeded to describe to me every funny detail of the *Seinfeld* episode he was watching. I laughed with him. (*Seinfeld* was not even on that night.)

Another time he was describing something he was seeing on the ceiling, and he was laughing. He said, "Oh, I just wish you could see this."

"I wish that I could too," I replied, and I laughed with him.

Richard died after a nine-month fight. When he passed away it was hard. The entire situation seemed surreal. I was in shock for the better part of a year, but I was grateful for the memories of the laughter we had shared together during a difficult time.

Today, five years later, I am happy to report that I met a wonderful man, an engineer, Jim Duvander. He is a singer and was in chorus with me. We went on our first date to a movie. I was a bit embarrassed as I was crying at the end, but out of the corner of my eye I could see his tears, too. He has a tender spirit and is a man of faith. His wife had passed away from cancer, just as my husband had. We fell in love and were married. We spend lots of our time together laughing and finding humor in our lives. We both know there is a marvelous power in humor.

Paula juggling.

Paula Duvander

Chapter 5

THE GIFT OF TRIALS

We all have things that happen to us in our lives that bring us great sorrow, yet we spend our lives searching for the things that will make us happy. Over time I've learned that trials and sorrows can help us in our quest for happiness and teach us how to turn our scars into stars.

I once read a wonderful essay about a quest for happiness. It inspired me to adapt some of the thoughts:

The concept was based on a little girl riding a Ferris wheel with her mommy by her side. The girl was absolutely thrilled and enthralled with the excitement of the ride. As she went way up into the air with the seat swaying back and forth, she listened to the music of the steam calliope and watched the twinkling colored lights that make a Ferris wheel appear to be a veritable fairy land of joy and happiness. She squealed to her mother, "Mommy, isn't this wonderful? Aren't you happy?"

"Oh, yes," the mother answered with little or no feeling, for she was thinking of a travel poster advertising to her that happiness is certainly not here but is definitely in another place—far away.

Many of us seem to live our lives looking for happiness. That is not always a bad thing, but it can be if we continually believe that happiness is someplace else and not in the present. Dr. James Dobson suggests that if we think another set of circumstances can make us happy, we should think again! The grass may look greener on the other side of the fence, but it still has to be mowed. Many times life involves days made up of monotony. For some women it's carpools, babies, diapers, grocery shopping, sack lunches, washing dishes, and endless lists of chores. For others, it's a long commute, countless meetings, lunch at the same deli every day, sore feet, and endless lists of chores once the sun goes down and we walk through the front door. Our minds trick us into thinking that if we could get away from the monotony for a little while, then we would be happy.

There are three ways that Satan can tempt us to veer off course. These temptations are (1) Inappropriate pleasure—to have what seems to be a little innocent fun, which could be the beginning of something destructive. (2) Romance—some tender touch or affection, which seems to fill a need in our lives. (3) Ego needs—someone to admire us, pay attention, and make us feel valued.

Think of the man who has a fling with his secretary and believes his life will soon be all pleasure and romance and that his ego needs will be boosted by this new and pleasurable distraction. The affair might continue, causing one marriage to end and another to begin. Soon, the man will find out that his new life has reverted back to the same. Or, he might find that his new life of deception and sneaking around can be more exhausting and stressful than the unexciting life from which he escaped. Either way, he'll still find that green grass always has to be mowed. However, if he instead decided to skip the affair altogether, to put the romance back into his marriage, to find ways to give others pleasure, and to feed others' egos, he might find that mowing his green lawn is somewhat relaxing and maybe even something to be proud of every week. Certainly, he'll have fewer problems in the long run.

Or how about the young woman who "knows" that if she can just find Prince Charming, he will light up her life and make everything she's worrying about now just disappear. She eventually does find an eternal companion, and there is light, but not all the time. There are still times where she feels very dark. So, she says, "I know what will light up my life—children." Sometimes children can be so overwhelming that she still gets short-circuited. The lights are not always on. She sinks into a form of despair because it troubles her that everything isn't always perfect—as she believes it should be. Soon, she starts missing out on the little moments that could brighten her day and keep her going during the dark times.

Or how about the woman who thinks shopping (read: acquiring more things) will provide the happiness she's been searching for? I've definitely been that woman. I remember one day going into an antique shop and finding a set of red velvet drapes. Oh, they were perfect for my home. But I could not afford them. When I talked to the owner of the store, he made a deal with me. He had a huge coffee table from Mexico. He wanted it gold leafed. I knew how to do gold leafing. It took me months because it was so large and detailed. But I did it. The red velvet drapes were mine. I hung them with great excitement, only to discover that each pleat was faded and had moth holes. Oh, they were such a disappointment. They certainly did not light up my life. If only I had really looked at them and measured them and pictured them in my living room to make sure they were indeed the perfect antidote before making my decision.

Expecting to receive happiness from other people, places, and new things will never light up our lives. We actually already have the light within us that will give us everything we want. It is the light of Christ. It is always lit, always there. The secret of true happiness is when we let that Christlike light shine through us to others.

Whatever happens in our lives, we have the ability to choose our reaction to it. You can be better or bitter. You can make your trials stumbling blocks or stepping stones. So why not chose the better way?

Learn the Lessons. If we let the Lord into our lives, we can, in our grief and struggles, find some reasons for what happens. I've heard it said, "No pain, no gain." I truly believe that real pain in our lives can bring us genuine love and humility—certainly a true gain. Of course, we would not choose pain, but when it comes, know that it will not be in vain. If we are willing, we can be taught lessons during those times.

When I was younger, I had some truly tragic events happen. I was seventeen when I went to New York City to become a ballerina. I was called into the office one day at the New York City Ballet Company and was told I needed to lose weight. A side effect of my efforts to diet was that I became anorexic and bulimic.

Then, as I related in chapter 1, at age nineteen I married a man who was manic-depressive. I lived through twelve years of an abusive marriage. Eventually my husband took his own life. I was left to raise two small children by myself. I married my second husband, a wonderful man, and my family joined the Church. My children were raised in the Church, and I started magnifying my talent for speaking. I could have been tempted to say, "Thank goodness, all of my troubles are behind me now." But, just when it seemed like life was perfect something else would happen to cause me pain. Of course, with this pain always came valuable life lessons.

Several years ago, I had a challenge that almost ruined my life. It started out so simply. I was asked to speak at a nearby high school. The school had some horrendous problems. The administrators were fighting Satanism and sexual harassment problems. A new superintendent had come in, and she was determined to change things. She got death threats and even had to have a bodyguard. She asked me to come and speak in my capacity as one who trains beauty queens. They even offered to pay for the flight if one of my beauty queens would come. I agreed. I wanted to help.

The day arrived. Since it was a public high school, and they didn't know me, I needed to think of an opening for my talk that would get their attention and let them know that I would be fun to listen to. I had seen a young man at an Especially for Youth talent show do a comedy skit, eating a banana to the music from *2001: A Space Odyssey*. It looked hilarious and would certainly grab their attention.

I was in the middle of this huge auditorium in front of hundreds of teenagers. With a great deal of drama, I naively peeled the banana and started eating it to the rhythm of the music. They were yelling and hollering and laughing, totally undisciplined. At the end of my talk, when Erica Havig, who was Miss Montana, stood and walked to the front of the stage, two smart-aleck boys bumped her, trying to push her off onto the floor. It was not a nice experience for either of us.

A week later, a man from the school called and said, "I think you should get a lawyer."

"What?" I asked. "Why do I need a lawyer?"

Apparently three teachers were about to be fired. One of them had made a video of my talk and had removed the sound of the music and laughter and cut the video to look pornographic. He sent it to a television station, which asked to interview me so that I could issue a public apology. I called a lawyer, but this incident made the news locally and nationally.

There are no words to express to you how I felt. I was totally innocent, but there was no one to go to bat for me. What was circulating was a twisted, evil version of the event. I was asked not to speak anymore. It was the biggest nightmare I have ever been through in my life. How could this happen?

I was in pain. I was furious. How dare somebody accuse me of something so atrocious? The last thing in the world I would do is a pornographic act in front of hundreds of teenagers. How could Heavenly Father let that happen to me? I kept asking. Why do I have to go through this when all I'm trying to do is serve?

At first my husband said, "We'll bring a lawsuit." We were going to sue the school board and the teacher who had edited the video. Then we thought about it some more. And, like Tevye in *Fiddler on the Roof* (Stein, 1971), we came to the realization that an eye for an eye and a tooth for a tooth would leave us blind and toothless. Hard as it was, I decided to rise above it. I decided to take the high road and do something good and positive since I had to drop out of speaking in the United States. I would give it some time and try to find the "gift" within the trial.

Still, questions nagged at me: Why was this happening to me? Why had Heavenly Father let me down? I went to the temple questioning. I couldn't believe how abandoned I felt. I closed my eyes and said, "Heavenly Father, are you there?"

I heard a small voice in my head saying, "Yes, Barbara, I'm here."

Then with my eyes closed, I felt a white light as bright as diamonds or sunlight glistening on the water. It was so brilliant. I knew at that moment, sitting there in the temple, that Heavenly Father and Jesus Christ knew what I was going through. They loved me.

I walked out of the temple that day with no obligations ahead of me. I decided to visit my parents, especially since my father's birthday was coming up. I hadn't been able to visit my parents in several years due to my heavy speaking schedule. They lived several thousand miles away. But the moment I walked into their house, I realized that there were serious problems. I discovered that my mother had dementia, which turned out to be Alzheimer's. She had become incontinent. Their entire house reeked of urine and feces. There were cockroaches everywhere. I felt sick inside.

I asked Dad, "How can you live like this?"

He said, "Oh, you know your mother would never leave here."

I took my dad to lunch and persuaded him to look at a retirement home. It was very nice. When we came back, there on the driveway, right outside the screen door, was my mother lying on the ground. She had blacked out or fallen.

I jumped out of the car and ran to her. "Mother, are you okay?"

She turned her hand to show me her watch. She said, "I've been lying here for three hours." It was 110 degrees in El Paso, Texas, that day. She was lying on the concrete in the blazing sun.

We called the paramedics, and she was taken to the hospital. They told us they would have to amputate her leg.

Like one possessed, I cleaned out my parents' home, full of fifty years of accumulated things. I gave items away. We had a garage sale. I put their house on the market. I went back and forth to the hospital. I moved my dad and bought him furniture more appropriate for the assisted living center.

One night, at about two o'clock in the morning, I was driving back to my hotel feeling absolutely exhausted! The realtor was coming the next morning. I said a quick prayer. "Heavenly Father, I'm so grateful that I have had the time to be here." I was flooded with the feeling that Heavenly Father was telling me that this was the only way to get my attention and let me see the priorities in my life.

My mother didn't have to have her leg amputated. What a great relief! My parents moved into the retirement home, but my mom never did really get back to where she had been. She needed the care the center provided. It was sad, but I was able to be with them through that transition. I know that sometimes things happen for a reason. We don't know whether it's physical pain or mental trials from which we can learn and grow. Hopefully you'll be able to turn back someday, as I have, and say, "I understand. Thank you."

I called my dad every day and traveled back and forth often. That summer my daughter got married, and my mother wanted so much to go to the wedding. She couldn't, of course, because she was in the hospital. After Wendy and Shane's temple marriage, we all flew to El Paso and took the wedding party to my mother in the hospital. When my daughter walked into my mother's hospital room in her wedding dress, it was a very special moment for everyone. It was the greatest service project I could have done for my mother's happiness.

With the passage of a little time, the incident with my speaking in the local high school was forgotten, and I resumed my speaking schedule, but with a great deal more attention to my family.

The scriptures tell us that a man plans his course, but the Lord determines his steps (see Proverbs 16:9). When things go wrong, you realize that the world isn't going to devote itself to making you happy. You have to begin to move forward again. Life doesn't always turn out the way you plan. In Romans, Paul wrote, "Whensoever I take my journey into Spain, I will come to you" (Romans 15:24). He didn't make it to Spain. Instead, he was thrown into prison. But it was in prison that he wrote the epistles.

My grandmother used to remind me that every trial has a silver lining. I believe that. One of those silver linings is that while we are going through hard times, we do not have to go through them by ourselves. We can turn to Christ. Jesus made us a promise that He would take our burdens. "Come unto me all ye that labour and are heavy laden, and I will give you rest. Take my yoke upon you, and learn of me; for I am meek and lowly in heart: and ye shall find rest unto your souls. For my yoke is easy, and my burden is light" (Matthew 11:28–30). He truly understands our despair and pain. And He will always be there.

It is our Lord and Savior who said, "Be patient in afflictions, for thou shalt have many; but endure them, for, lo, I am with thee, even unto the end of thy days" (Doctrine and Covenants 24:8). With Christ by our side it will be easier to endure, for He is the silver lining within our trials.

I met Jodi (her name has been changed) at BYU–Hawaii. A meeting just for the two of us had been arranged. As I sat with her, I could hardly believe the inconceivable, magnanimous story of forgiveness I was hearing. What a remarkable young mother this was. She had served a mission, been married in the temple, and had twin daughters. With her marriage over, her husband having married her best friend, she was now living alone. She was trying so diligently to raise her daughters and go to school. I felt nothing but admiration for her striving attitude.

I lost track of Jodi, but I recently heard from her after four years, and the end of her story is like a fairytale. I share it here with her permission.

JODI'S STORY

(All names in this story have been changed.)

My mom and I had a terrible relationship throughout my growing-up years. Sometimes she wouldn't speak to me for days. My dad didn't know how to be a dad either. My parents never attended any events throughout my school years; but, I love my parents.

When I was nine years old, I began running because I thought I was fat. When I weighed 120 pounds as a teenager, my dad said I was heavy and should lose weight; I became bulimic and an obsessive runner. I tried every diet there was, from diet pills to starving myself. At nineteen I was so thin, my stepmom made me see her doctor. He immediately said, "You are going to the hospital."

I went to the hospital for an eating disorder for six weeks. While in the hospital, I saw a girl that weighed seventy-one pounds. She literally looked like a walking skeleton. That had an effect on me like no other I can describe. I told the doctor, "I don't need to be here."

He replied, "Jodi, you are in denial, and you need to be here more than the seventy-one-pound skeleton girl." They taught me that an eating disorder is not a problem with food but something deeper. For me it was poor self-worth, no self-esteem. In some ways it was the best six weeks of my life. I felt God guiding my life, and it helped me see the beauty in myself. I became the healthiest that I had ever been. To this day I have good eating and exercising patterns that I know will last a lifetime. What seemed to be one of the greatest trials in my life at that time, turned out to be one of the greatest blessings.

When my mom saw the change in me, she looked back over her indifference to me through my childhood years, she felt that she had failed.

She hadn't failed. She had taught me the gospel! I love my mother, and we have grown close through the years.

After high school, I attended Brigham Young University and graduated in pre-medicine. When I was twenty-one, I went on a mission to the Florida Tallahassee Mission. I learned to depend on the Lord for everything. I broke the record for the number of baptisms in my mission.

I met my husband briefly on my mission. I had been home for three months when he looked me up. We fell head over heels in love right away. We dated for three months and were married three days after Christmas in the Cardston Alberta Temple. This was a dream come true. I had served my mission, and now I had my temple marriage. I always lived right and stayed close to the Lord. I was the happiest I had ever been and felt oh so lucky.

Our marriage started to crumble. I needed and craved affection because my parents had never given it to me. My husband didn't give affection either. I always thought our marriage was going to work out somehow until the day he said, "Well, divorce is always an option."

My husband had grown up in Calgary, and his best friend's wife and I were friends from high school. I was a genuine and true friend that she could trust. I truly loved her grandmother and her family, too. When our friends were married, my husband was the best man, and I was a bridesmaid for Tanya. We were best friends as couples. We even had each other's wedding pictures on our mantles.

I had a difficult pregnancy and was in the hospital for six weeks. My husband came to the hospital every night faithfully. I felt like this was a bonding time, and I treasured it. We were blessed with twin daughters.

My husband was a business consultant and traveled a lot. When the twins were three months old, he finally told me the truth about what went on while he was traveling. He was involved in drugs, alcohol, women, and so on. Our marriage was nothing more than a lie.

In the meantime, I was trying to deal with being a new mom and had all of the cares of running our home. At the same time, my husband's friend (Tanya's husband) was having severe problems with depression. My husband, as his best friend, was aware of the problems. We decided to plan a little couples' getaway.

The day before we were to leave, our friend drove to the beach with his gun and took his own life. His wife was five months' pregnant. As soon as we heard the tragic news, we drove over to their home, and the three of us just sat on the couch crying, talking, and trying to comfort each other. We sat there in the same spot for literally thirty-six hours straight. I finally fell asleep.

When I awakened in the middle of the night, I saw Tanya in my husband's arms. He was caressing her face with his hand and kissing her tenderly all over her face while whispering to her. I thought to myself, "This must be a nightmare. My best friend's husband just killed himself, and now my husband is giving his friend's wife the tenderness and caring I've craved and desired my entire life." I immediately shut my eyes and fell back into an exhausted sleep, but I knew our marriage was over.

After a few months, Tanya's baby was due, and my husband suggested we go to the hospital to be a support for her. I didn't want to go, but he said we should go to be supportive. We agreed to go, and he promised we would stay together. We went in together, but he left me to be with her in the delivery room. I ended up in the waiting room alone with Tanya's family and feeling completely humiliated.

At Christmas, my husband finally left. We got a divorce, and he sold our home. Our home and neighborhood were the children's stability. I

THE GIFT OF TRIALS

moved to Utah to start a new life. I had a good education. I had graduated from BYU in pre-medicine, but as I weighed my possibilities of being
a breadwinner in any of those fields, I knew I would not have flexibility
with my schedule.

After an interesting conversation with a pilot, he suggested that I
train to become a pilot. He told me not to let my being a woman stop me.
A light-bulb went on, and the Spirit spoke to me plainly and clearly that
night. I enrolled in flight school in Arizona and moved within three weeks.
I had no idea how difficult this task would be. School started out with
twelve students and lasted three years. At the end, there were only two of
us left. I am a very determined person, and I endure to the end. I may get
discouraged, but I pick myself back up and go another day. Taking apart
carburetors, learning aerodynamics, understanding the weather, studying
the books, this was all easier than the stress of flying itself. My stepdad,
who is a pilot, said, "In all truthfulness, female pilots are better than we
men are because they are multi-taskers. Jodi, you will be a great pilot."

Now that I am finished with commercial pilot school, I can look back
and say, "You've come a long way." It was hard to continue when others
were dropping out of class like flies. I found that it helped to have a partner to help you through, and my partner has always been my Heavenly
Father. I can depend on Him for everything. It was that way in my childhood, during my teen years, my college days, on my mission, and so on.

My ex-husband and my friend Tanya were married three months after
our divorce. They asked me to move back to Canada so that my children
could be close to their father. They would help me get settled into an
apartment where the girls could be in school close to both of our homes.
I knew it would be best for our children emotionally to have both parents

in their lives and for them to see everyone happy, but nonetheless this was a difficult decision.

I moved to Calgary so that my children could have both mom and dad close by. I prayed to Heavenly Father for guidance in all that I did. I was hurt, and I knew that Tanya was hurting, too. My friend felt awful for what she had done. Even more so since I had forgiven her. I felt that she must have been caught up in an awful situation. Her emotions were sorrowful and confused since she was mourning the loss of her husband. She was pregnant, not a member of the Church, and her lack of knowledge had left her crippled.

Life must go on! Heavenly Father told me, "Make peace." For my own soul and happiness and that of my children, I have concentrated on finding a new life and occupation that allows me to spend my off-work hours with my children. How blessed I am to be in a location where my children can be with their father when I am away flying, and home with me full-time when I am home, and to have a friend for their stepmom who loves them and treats my children as her own. I have made it a priority to hold no grudges and to place my children first.

I met Mark in flight school. He was so handsome, but the best thing was how much he loved my daughters and how much they loved him. One day, after we had been dating for a while, I picked up my girls from school, and they had a treasure map that Mark obviously had created and given to them. It led me to all my favorite places until we ended up at the airport with a plane waiting, with Mark as our pilot, to take all of us to a secluded restaurant. Flowers were everywhere. My girls were excited with the adventure as the courses of dinner were served. Dessert came with balloons attached. The girls were told to pop their balloons. Inside was another note leading them to the treasure. He had a ruby bracelet for one, and a ruby necklace for the other, and then he got down on his knee in front of my girls and asked them if he could marry their mother. They replied with cheers. I popped my balloon and out came my ring. We were married in the Cardston Alberta Temple. "And it came to pass that we lived after the manner of happiness" (2 Nephi 5:27).

I am so grateful to Heavenly Father that my life has been blessed with a man who truly loves me, and I am unbelievably happy. Heavenly Father heard my prayers. With His help, I was able to completely forgive and make peace as He asked me to do. He has helped me to fulfill my dream of becoming an airline pilot, and He has blessed me with the ability to see the gift that is within the trial.

Chapter 6

THE GIFT OF JOY

L ife-changing inspiration comes at the oddest moments and in the
most unusual ways. I didn't realize that such a simple phrase—joy in
the journey—would affect me so greatly.

I have been profoundly moved by the idea that in our life's journey
there is a constantly unfolding plan for good. Just by living one day at a
time with excitement and enthusiasm, always looking for the good, and
trusting in the Lord, we will find joy. And that joy brings us peace and the
knowledge that there is order in the plan of our lives, even through difficulties and tragedies.

Let me explain how that phrase became so important to me. I am a
speaker at youth events such as the Especially for Youth (EFY) programs
sponsored by Brigham Young University. And I've been a director of youth
programs for other organizations for many years. One year, as we were
preparing for the upcoming theme for EFY, I opened the packet of information that was sent to that year's speakers. I read the title—Joy in the
Journey.

Barbara dances leading role in "Emé Vous Bach" (I Love Bach)

"How nice," I thought, "I really love that theme." I then looked up the scripture meant to accompany the theme. It was Doctrine and Covenants 100:12, "Therefore, continue your journey and let your hearts rejoice; for behold, and lo, I am with you even unto the end."

"Continue your journey . . . let your heart rejoice . . . I am with you." My heart was receptive. The beauty and power of the words and their meaning began to work in my mind.

At that time in my life, I was facing some health problems and personal losses that were challenging my ability to do the things I knew the Lord wanted me to do. Because of the wear and tear on my hip joints from years as a ballerina, I had degenerative arthritis. I started having a lot of pain, and was on pain medication and limping constantly.

The following month, the doctor said I needed surgery. It should have been a simple procedure, but after the procedure, I stood and fell to the floor. I said, "I have no feeling in my legs." They had accidentally pinched my sciatic nerve.

At that moment, I could not quite see the joy in this particular journey. But I was allowed to go home with the promise that the numbness would wear off in a few hours.

About 3:00 in the morning, I woke up and got out of bed to go to the bathroom. I collapsed to the floor. I still had no feeling in one leg. I sat there on the floor with the words to an EFY theme song going through my head, "so everyday we put our faith in heaven, and in the light of the morning we find strength to rise again" ("Joy in the Journey," Tyler Castleton, et al. Used with permission.). Through my tears, I promised the Lord that I would honor all my commitments, even if I had to do so in a wheelchair.

I struggled back to bed, and the next morning I did get the feeling back in my leg. But something was not right. The pain in my leg continued to worsen. In the next few months, I was using a cane. Then I had to be in a wheelchair while directing the Academy for Girls program.

In the middle of the week I spent at Academy for Girls, I received a telephone call from my sister, Paula. She told me that our mother had passed away. Our mother had been in a rest home suffering with Alzheimer's for about eight years. It was the really the best thing, but still it was a huge shock. It's true that no matter how old you are, you never get over the loss of your mother. We had lost our father the previous year. I couldn't hold back the tears; I felt so alone.

I had no time to recover from the phone call. I was scheduled to teach 180 teenage girls about learning to be the kind of person that builds others. My mother was just that kind of person. So I proceeded to talk about my mother, a most incredible woman, who knew how to build people up.

My mother knew how to find joy in the journey. She had incredible and wide-ranging talents. She could look at a picture of a suit in a magazine, cut a pattern, and make it. She was a fashion model, and she had her pilot's license. But what she is remembered for was her talent for making people feel wonderful about themselves.

The day I was informed of my mother's death, I told those teenage girls this story, which illustrated my mother's ability to build others:

Whenever we went out to eat in our hometown, she often complimented the waitresses. One day she told our server, "You're the best waitress in all of El Paso, Texas." Then she went home, opened her file, and took out a blank award certificate that you can purchase in a stationery store. She filled it out, writing, "To Maria Gonzales, the best waitress in all of El Paso, Texas." She then signed it with her name, Hilda Harrell.

I said, "Mother, who are you? You're nobody, and you're giving this lady an award?"

She didn't care what I thought of her idea. She then proceeded to cut out paper roses and decorate the certificate. Everything she did had paper roses on it. It was just her trademark, I guess. She then mailed the certificate to the restaurant.

Then it was my turn to be surprised. The next time I went to that restaurant, there hanging on the wall behind the cash register, in a frame, was Mother's award certificate.

I said to the cashier, "Oh, it looks like one of your waitresses was named the best waitress."

The cashier said, "Yes, she received this award. She was named out of all the waitresses in El Paso."

I had to smile. That was my mother.

I continued to tell the girls similar stories, including this one: When I was about fourteen, Mother was a volunteer at our local hospital. One day she came home and said that she was going to make one of the ladies in the hospital a Hospital Queen. And I was going to be the official photographer.

Like a typical teenager, I was mortified. "Mother, you can't do that. It's so dorky."

She sent me to the garage to rummage around and find some artificial roses. I dusted them off. She told me to put a red ribbon around them, and she made a poster with the words *Hospital Queen* stenciled on it. And, of course, she decorated it with cut-out paper roses. She even made a paper crown and a sash of white ribbon where she had written "Hospital Queen" in glue and sprinkled glitter on it. I took the Polaroid camera, and off we went to the hospital.

The first patient selected was someone my mother knew. She opened the door to her room. There was this woman, ill and hooked to an IV. Mother hustled in and announced, "You have been chosen Hospital Queen!" Mother was quite dramatic (I know where I get it from), and she put up the poster. She arranged the paper crown on the patient's head, draped the sash across her hospital gown, and gave her the red roses to hold, and said, "Here is our official photographer."

I clicked the camera, handed her the photo, and got out of there as quickly as possible.

We did this for a week, selecting several women to be Hospital Queen. A short time later, I was following Mother down the hall, about ten paces behind, literally dragging my feet. As we passed the room of one of the women we had selected as Hospital Queen, I heard this woman's daughter talking on the phone.

The one-sided conversation that I overheard went something like this: "Susan, you'll never believe this, but my mother was chosen as Hospital Queen. Yes, the whole hospital. She received a crown and a bunch of roses. We even have a picture. I had thirty copies made. I'm sending them to all the relatives. The doctor said it just boosted her spirits, and she is going home tomorrow."

I was amazed. That's when I understood that my mother was a builder. She was like that until the very end, even when Alzheimer's had taken much of her mind, her instinct to reach out and build others was still there. One lady at the rest home where Mother was being cared for said that one day she received a little scrap of paper on which my mother had shakily written "award," for having the best wreath on her door.

I finished telling the story of my mother to all these teenage girls. Then I told them that I had just received news that my mother had died and that I would be leaving at the end of the week to go to her funeral. The girls were wonderful. They cried and hugged me. It was truly joyful. Before I left, these girls made awards for everyone—the cafeteria staff, the people in the offices, everyone. It was so touching, I cried on the plane all the way to Texas.

When I arrived, it was wonderful to see my sister. We went to the funeral home, and I remember walking in and seeing Mother's casket. I just stopped dead in my tracks. Previously, I had chosen a beautiful bronze casket with roses hand done on all four corners, but this casket was orange with no roses. Little things like that shouldn't make a difference, but in my emotional state, it seemed like this last tribute to our mother was ruined. My sister put her arm around me and assured me that everything would be okay.

That night, my sister, Paula, spent all night cutting out paper roses and pasting them on all four corners of the casket. I just broke into a smile when I saw it. Our mother would have loved it. The paper roses would have thrilled her. In that moment of great sorrow, that thoughtful gesture by my sister brought me joy, unexpected joy.

When we went to the gravesite, my daughter Wendy's little two-year-old boy, Taylor, got up and walked up to the casket. He poked a big Tigger sticker up on the casket, a Tigger sticker that said, "Bouncing for Joy." I could just see my mom smiling. There was joy in the journey—for her and for us.

Finding the Joy

I continued my speaking schedule, but my leg became progressively worse. By this time I was using two canes and was on pain medication much of the time. As I struggled to keep my commitments, I finally reached the point where I could not go on. The doctor took X-rays and said, "All the blood supply has been cut off. Your hip is disintegrating. If you try to go on, you may never walk again."

I entered the hospital and had surgery almost immediately. I had to have a total hip replacement. At the end of the surgery, I remember coming out of the anesthesia and thinking it had taken at least a year of constant pain to get to that day.

My friend, Amanda Dupont, came to see me in the hospital. I told her, "Amanda, I did find joy in the journey. I don't know how, but I felt the Spirit of the Lord helping me through every speaking assignment and all the physical pain."

Amanda said something that affected my entire way of thinking. She asked, without waiting for me to answer, "How have you been able to have the Spirit with you all that time? How have you gone through all the pain

medication where sometimes you couldn't even think straight?" And then she looked at me and continued as she was patting my hand, "Oh, my dear, don't you see. All that time He carried you."

Barbara tosses her crutches into the ocean.

Now I know that He will always be there giving joy in the moments of great sorrow. It is within these moments that we will find our most precious treasures scattered along this road of our journey. We must look for the good, and we must find moments for gratitude. For some the tragedy of life can be overwhelming, even beyond comprehension. But we have been promised that in the darkest moments, when we can no longer go on in our own strength, He will carry us. It is in those moments that a small light pierces the blackness of despair. And hope continues.

I met Sharon Duke when I gave a talk for the company at which she was an employee. After the talk she came up and told me her story. I couldn't believe what she had gone through already and what incredible trials were facing her in the future, yet she was so positive, so happy, and so helpful to me. We have become good friends over the years, and to me she is my greatest example of a woman who truly has found the gift of joy. This is her story, printed with her permission:

My dear friend Sharon

SHARON'S STORY

As a young girl, I often dreamed of what my life would be like when I was all grown up. I dreamed of the perfect man—a prince—and a house full of children. We would be rich and live in a mansion. I would have maids and a gardener. We would travel the world in our own airplane and give things to those in need. I would be able to give treasures to my parents and family, things that we never had as I grew up. My life would be perfect.

The dreams of that young girl faded quickly into reality as the years passed. But I do believe that my life now is better than any dream I ever conjured up as a freckle-faced little girl. I do not live in a mansion or own an airplane. I do my own gardening, and the gifts I give to my family and those in need come from within me in the love I can offer. Life's greatest treasures are the joys that come from watching my children and from growing with a true prince, my husband, Ken, on our journey through life.

Ken is a remarkable man. He runs six days a week and will complete his twenty-second marathon this fall. He mows the lawn, does dishes and laundry, vacuums, and helps with things that most men consider women's work. He is patient, loving, and can be romantic when he tries really hard. I cannot let him work in the garden because he pulls up all my flowers. He loves to use the weed-eater, a real man's tool, but I won't let him do that either.

Ken can't see my flowers in the garden. He is blind. There are many things Ken cannot do, but he chooses to focus on the things he can do. With the help of a few great friends, he is able to run like the wind. It is his freedom from a world of darkness. A positive outlook has enabled Ken to function as normally as possible. He takes the bus to and from work every day. He works as an information systems manager and programmer, thus supporting his family's needs. I am grateful for his life and the choice he makes to see things through his heart.

Ken and I are blessed with five beautiful children. All were born by Caesarean section, three of them preemies. They are smart and talented in many ways. Our oldest, Eric, is a bright young man with wit and charm. Eric has a 40 percent hearing loss. I thought as he began the teen years that he suffered from selective hearing. It seemed he didn't need to listen to me anymore. But then, on a hunch, I had his hearing tested. I sat outside the chamber where the hearing test took place, hoping for some kind of confirmation that my suspicions were wrong. The emotion and tears came fast and furious as the series of beeps went unheard. I wanted him to raise his hand so badly when a beep sounded. I became numb as the doctor tried to explain what was happening. There was no explanation for the loss. "Perhaps it is related to his premature birth," I was told. No answers, no cure.

We went home. I remember feeling the fog that surrounded me the next few weeks. I wanted to blame myself. It didn't take too long before Eric gave me a precious gift—a valuable lesson. He informed me matter-of-factly that he would be just fine. He would cope with this challenge and move on with life. If his dad could live without sight, he could live with a hearing loss. Blessings flowed into our lives on waves of light. We would, after all, be okay.

My second child, an angel from heaven, was born in March. I had developed toxemia again with my pregnancy, just like my first. I received a prompting that something was wrong on that chilly spring day. I called the doctor and promptly followed his instructions to go to the hospital. I had hoped for a vaginal birth, and the idea of another C-section was torment for me. I was hooked to monitors that checked the stress level on my daughter. It seemed only a few minutes before I was being wheeled down the hall toward the operating room. How could this be happening again? I wondered. Why couldn't I do this birth thing right?

I prayed for my daughter. I hoped all would be well. An incision was made, and with a few tugs and pulls, she was out. "She is pink but tiny," the doctor said. I waited. The silence in the busy operating room was deafening to me. I knew something was not right. In a daze, I heard the news, and a tiny baby was placed in my hand, which was tied to the operating table. It was there she took her last sigh of breath. In a whirlwind of emotion, my daughter entered back into the presence of our Heavenly Father.

The room was still, and I felt perfect peace. Spiritual arms held me tight, and I was blessed with the comforting knowledge that this was the Lord's will. She was given the name of Krystina Kareen before she left us. I later learned she weighed only two pounds. The dull ache of her absence is still with me to this day. Our family has been so sweetly blessed by having an angel watching over us. I do not mourn for her, because she has asked me not to. I do look forward to the day I will meet her again. For now, she teaches others and blesses our lives. Heaven is not so far away.

Brandon, my third child, is almost fifteen. He was a normal weight at birth, and I rejoiced when I was able to take a baby home without a lengthy hospital stay for him. He is a computer whiz and keeps us, his parents, on our toes.

Allysha is twelve. What a blessing to have her in our lives. She was diagnosed with retinitis pigmentosa a few years ago. This is the same disease her father has. She too will eventually be blind. Allysha loves to read, dance, sing, nurture animals, and is blessed with many talents. Again, we try to focus on abilities rather than a future we can't predict. We find such happiness and joy in each day together.

My youngest child, Jacob, is almost eight. He too was premature at birth, weighing just over three pounds. He spent four weeks in the hospital before coming home at four pounds. The decision was made during his birth that it would not be safe for me to have any other children. I had done my part the best I could. It was time to let go of that part of my life.

It was soon after having Jacob that I began to experience tremendous abdominal pain. One Sunday, I could bear the pain no more and went to the emergency room. I was suffering from pancreatitis. I stayed in the hospital for one week on IVs and no food. The night I ate solid food for the first time, the pain returned. The decision was made to have surgery.

Less than six months later, the pancreatitis returned. I had a radical procedure next, hoping that things would get better.

Several months later, I began having pain. I again went under the knife. I have had many episodes of pancreatitis the last few years. I feel the pain coming on, quit eating, and call the doctor. I know in my heart it will probably take my life someday, but for now, at this moment, I am well and happy. I will never give up without a fight.

When Brandon became ill with pancreatitis last year, I questioned why things like this continued to happen. The answer is always the same. We must always continue to find joy in our journey and endure to the end. Embrace all that life has to offer. A positive attitude is the best medicine for any trial that comes along.

I get through some of the toughest moments only by the tender love that comes through a loving Father in Heaven and my Savior, Jesus Christ. I have learned that the key to finding peace in this world is to have simple, unquestioning faith. We cannot control our world or circumstances. We can believe that we have the power within us to endure and find the gift of joy in all that comes our way.

Chapter 7

THE GIFT OF
SELF-WORTH

Life is not a journey to the grave with the intention of arriving without incident, in a pretty, well-preserved body. Instead, I hope we all skid in broadside, thoroughly used up, totally worn out, and loudly proclaiming, "Wow, Heavenly Father, what a ride!" One day I hope we arrive before the throne of God with a huge smile on our faces from the wonderful lives we have lived. We know that we will take with us the attitude we had in life. In Mormon 9:14 it says, "He that is happy shall be happy still; and he that is unhappy shall be unhappy still."

I've read that only one in five women feel good about themselves. Not feeling good about ourselves comes from many sources. One of the biggest sources is the media. We look at the advertisements and models in the magazines and compare ourselves to them. In reality, the facts of the matter are startling. Several years ago, an e-mail with the following statistics made its way to my desktop. I can't corroborate all of the facts, but most of them are fairly simple to prove:

- A 1995 psychological study found that three minutes spent looking at a fashion magazine caused 70 percent of women to feel depressed, guilty, and shameful.
- Models twenty years ago weighed 8 percent less than the average woman. Today they weigh 23 percent less. Models in the 60s wore a stock size 8/10. Today they are taller and wear a stock size 0/2.
- The models in the magazines are airbrushed—not perfect!
- There are three billion women who don't look like supermodels and only eight who do.
- If Barbie were a real woman, she'd have to walk on all fours due to her proportions.
- The average woman weighs 144 pounds, is 5 foot 3½ inches tall, and wears between a 12 and 14 dress size.
- Marilyn Monroe wore a size 14.

New York Times best-selling author Marianne Williamson writes: "If we truly believed in an internal light, we would not believe the power of external forces. . . . We would not be tempted to see hair and clothes and makeup as sources of so much of our self-esteem and the ideal beauty of a fashion model as a sign that we are not beautiful at all. In the words of Naomi Wolf, 'We as women are trained to see ourselves as cheap imitations of fashion photographs rather than seeing fashion photographs as cheap imitations of women.'

"But we are ultimately responsible for how we see ourselves. . . . We are glorious because we are not beings of this world at all. Our spiritual essence is nonmaterial, nonphysical; and when we become aware of this, we are genuinely empowered. When we are truly aware of our spiritual glory, a varicose vein or two is not that big a deal" (*A Woman's Worth*, 24–25).

I would add that when we are truly aware of our spiritual glory, these futile comparisons will fall by the wayside, and we will blossom into the women that God truly meant us to be.

I have been speaking to women for more than twenty years. And I know personally that low self-esteem is the number one cause of depression and is of epidemic proportions worldwide. It seems depression is a burden many carry. And just the pace of life and the expectations placed on us take its toll.

Women don't like what they see in the mirror anymore. We are exhausted from a voluminous amount of daily tasks. We are lonely and bored. The romance, in many cases, seems to have ended. Some say to me, "I just wish I could feel beautiful again!" I look into the eyes of these women, and the light is gone. They seem ready to shout, "Is this all there is? Where is the joy?"

Singer/songwriter Julie de Azevedo wrote some beautiful lyrics to a song that captures this feeling:

> *Overwhelmed and underpaid*
> *Morning comes too soon*
> *Running late and on my plate*
> *A million things to do*
> *Got a baby cryin'*
> *Another trying to find the other shoe*
> *When I open my eyes*
> *The dam will break*
> *Their need will flood my room . . .*

[But Lord, you are the miracle-worker, so please]
Make enough of me to go around.
("Make Enough of Me"
Used with permission.)

Even the wife of a prophet of God, Marjorie Pay Hinckley, shared some of these same feelings: "I was just sure the first ten years would be bliss. But during our first year together I discovered . . . there were a lot of adjustments. Of course, they weren't the kind of thing you ran home to mother about. But I cried into my pillow now and again. The problems were almost always related to learning to live on someone else's schedule and to do things someone else's way. We loved each other, there was no doubt about that. But we also had to get used to each other. I think every couple has to get used to each other" (in Sheri Dew, *Go Forward with Faith,* 118).

As women, we tend to worry about everything. What if this happens? What if that happens? The scriptures tell us clearly that we need not fear. "For God hath not given us the spirit of fear; but of power, and of love, and of a sound mind" (2 Timothy 1:7). If God has not given us the spirit of fear, who has?

Satan. Fear is one of Satan's most powerful tools. It hampers us and keeps us from feeling the joy and happiness we should be experiencing in our lives. He wants us to be discouraged and overwhelmed. Fear makes us afraid of the future. Constant worry can sap our hope and our feelings of peace.

SATAN *VS.* OUR AGENCY

God does give us our agency, and it is in this freedom that Satan can use his cunning plans to cause us damage and harm.

He can twist our strengths and make them into weaknesses—but only with our permission. For example, he can take a woman's ability to do five things at once (multitasking) and turn it into something destructive—becoming overwhelmed. We often choose to take on too much by over scheduling ourselves to the point of exhaustion, a place where we can only see the negative. Unhappiness then creeps in, and we become sullen, never smiling, always tired, and eating junk foods filled with fats and sugar that give us false energy and comfort.

Satan can also take our God-given gift of sensitivity, which includes being loving, sympathetic, caring, compassionate, and kind, and with our consent he can turn that beautiful, God-given gift into depression using our sensitivities to allow us to feel wounded, offended, and bitter.

Criticism is one of Satan's favorite tools. Dr. John Gray, best-selling author of *Men Are from Mars, Women Are from Venus,* calls women the "home improvement committee," always seeking to change—and criticizing all along the way—those most dear to them (see p. 15). We need to understand what criticism can do and learn ways to change for the better.

Dr. John Lund, a most brilliant and witty LDS speaker, once gave an entire seminar on criticism, and for me it was a life-changing experience. Dr. Lund taught me that criticism is futile. It makes people instantly defensive, whether valid or not. If you want people to change, don't criticize. Dr. Lund challenged us to see if we could go twenty-for hours without criticizing anyone or anything, including ourselves.

I thought this would be easy because I'm a positive person. I walked out of the room, and I said to a friend, "Look at that lady. If only she had on a different color lipstick, she would look great."

It was not really mean-spirited. I felt it was in a spirit of helping—it was constructive criticism. Boy, was I wrong. As Dr. Lund had taught me, "Constructive means building up and criticism is tearing down. There is no such thing as constructive criticism."

Elder Callister says, "Many years ago an associate of mine decided he would please his wife by sharing with her a very specific compliment each night as he arrived home. One night he praised her cooking. A second night he thanked her for excellence in housekeeping. A third night he acknowledged her fine influence on the children. The fourth night, before he could speak, she said: 'I know what you are doing. I thank you for it. But don't say any of those things. Just tell me you think I am beautiful.'

"She expressed an important need that she had. Women ought to be praised for all the gifts they possess that so unselfishly add to the richness of our lives, including their attentiveness to their personal appearance" (Elder Douglas L. Callister, "Your Refined Heavenly Home," BYU Devotional, 19, Sept. 2006). We, as women, want to be loved, valued and appreciated.

My friend Bev Jones was a leader at girls' camp. During the counselor training, she came in with a cute new vest over her blouse. She opened her vest, and the inside was lined with sticky notes, all with the same phrase: "Please make me feel loved, important, and appreciated." She said, "This is all you need to do to be successful this week, and for the rest of your life."

President Gordon B. Hinckley said, "The women in our lives are creatures endowed with particular qualities, divine qualities, which cause them to reach out in kindness and with love to those about them. We can encourage that outreach if we will give them the opportunity to give expression to the talents and impulses that lie within them. In our old age my beloved companion said to me quietly one evening, 'You have always given me wings to fly, and I have loved you for it'" ("The Women in Our Lives," *Ensign*, November 2004, 84–85).

Most criticism comes from the outside, but change has to occur from within. Whether criticism is delivered verbally or non-verbally, the person to whom the criticism is directed will reject the person that is criticizing and will instantly start defending themselves whether the criticism was valid or not. Criticism is a not a motivator to your children, your husband, your friends, your employees, or your coworkers, but praise is.

Hatred, Judging, and Contention—More of Satan's Tools. I have watched twin boys for ten years who went through the divorce of their parents when they were in high school. These sweet boys were told about awful things that their father had done over the years while their mother had been true and faithful. For these ten years, the boys' hatred for their father has been growing. Now they only call him by his first name and say that after what he has done he is no longer their father. They never see or speak to him.

I agonize to see the bitterness that has poisoned their lives. The ancient philosopher Seneca said, "Anger is an acid that can do more harm to the vessel in which it is stored than to anything on which it is poured."

No matter the circumstances, we must forgive. God himself does not propose to judge man until the end of his days. Why then should we?

It says in the scriptures, "Vengeance is mine; I will repay, saith the Lord" (Romans 12:19). If you cannot forgive another person, you are making a mockery of the Atonement, and you have committed the greater sin. No matter what the situation we must forgive. The scriptures tell us to forgive. How many times? Seven? No, seventy times seven (see Matthew 18:21–22).

Satan's Most Destructive Plan. Sister Patricia T. Holland has said, "If I were Satan and wanted to destroy a society, I would stage a full-blown blitz on women. I would keep them so distraught and distracted that they would never find the calming strength and serenity for which their gender has always been known" (*On Earth as It Is in Heaven*, 85). Satan wants you to become so overwhelmed, overscheduled, and distracted that you will lose your divine focus and forget who you are. You are a daughter of God. You have a special mission to fulfill. You must stay positive and close to Him, constantly drawing on the power of heaven. You must seek His guidance and direction as you pray and read His word, and only then will your focus remain divine. However, the adversary is constantly working.

President Boyd K. Packer said, "The world grows increasingly noisy. . . . This trend to more noise, more excitement, more contention, less restraint, less dignity, less formality is not coincidental nor innocent nor harmless. The first order issued by a commander mounting a military invasion is the jamming of the channels of communications of those he intends to conquer" (*The Things of the Soul*, 92).

Busyness can overwhelm us. Having too much to do, being too tired to even pray—all symptoms of irreverence—"suits the purposes of the adversary by obstructing the delicate channels of communication," President Packer says. "Inspiration comes more easily in peaceful settings. Such words as *quiet, still, peaceable, Comforter,* abound in the scriptures: 'Be still, and know that I am God' (Psalm 46:10)" (*The Things of the Soul*, 92, 91). You must make time to pray, to be still, and to listen. God speaks softly—it is known as the still small voice.

Satan's plan is to try to twist your celestial traits (your strengths) and, with your agency, make them into weaknesses for your own self-destruction. He, with his numerous cunning impediments, tries to keep the channels of communication jammed with commotion and confusion or completely empty with deadly silence.

DO YOU REALLY KNOW WHO YOU ARE?

President Gordon B. Hinckley said, "Woman is God's supreme creation. . . . Of all the creations of the Almighty, there is none more beautiful, none more inspiring than a lovely daughter of God who walks in virtue with an understanding of why she should do so" ("Our Responsibility to Our Young Women," *Ensign,* September 1988, 11). On another occasion, he declared: "Rise above the dust of the world. Know that you are daughters of God. . . . Walk in the sun with your heads held high, knowing that you are loved and honored, and that you are part of a kingdom, and that there is for you a great work to be done which cannot be left to others" ("Live Up to Your Inheritance," *Ensign,* November 1983, 83–84).

I've heard it said that if you could envision the person God intended you to be, you would rise up and never be the same again.

Sometimes, I like to imagine that this scenario happens when we arrive in the next life:

On a table before us are two scrapbooks of our earthly journey. One is the scrapbook of your actual life on earth. The other is a scrapbook of what Heavenly Father had hoped for you to accomplish using the gifts, talents, and abilities He had given you before you left the premortal existence.

We will look at our earthly scrapbook and say, "Oh, yes, look, that is my wonderful husband and my children. There was our new home, and here are our . . ."

Heavenly Father softly answers, "But look over here at the other scrapbook, the life I had envisioned for you using the gifts and talents which I gave you." As He turns each page, you say, "Do you mean I could really have done that?"

He says, "I gave you all the gifts. I would have given you more direction if you had only asked. You weren't willing when opportunities arose to take a risk, to move out of your comfort zone, to better yourself.

"Before you left my side, I told you to 'seek ye earnestly the best gifts' (Doctrine and Covenants 46:8), and to 'neglect not the gift that is in thee' (1 Timothy 4:14)."

Dancer Eleanor Powell said, "What we are is a gift from God. What we become is our gift back to Him." You must do everything to reach your potential and become the person that Heavenly Father envisions you to be. No matter what your age, never quit trying, for you are His daughter.

Elder Jeffrey R. Holland said, "Be proud you are a woman. I want you to feel the reality of what that means, to know who you truly are. You are literally a spirit daughter of heavenly parents with a divine nature and an eternal destiny. . . . There could never be a greater authentication of your dignity, your worth, your privileges, and your promise. Your Father in Heaven knows your name and knows your circumstance. He hears your prayers. He knows your hopes and dreams, including your fears and frustrations. And He knows what you can become through faith in Him. Because of this divine heritage you . . . are empowered through obedience to become a rightful heir in His eternal kingdom. . . . Everything Christ taught He taught to women as well as men. . . . In the restored light of the gospel of Jesus Christ, a woman, including a young woman, occupies a majesty all her own in the divine design of the Creator" ("To Young Women," *Ensign*, November 2005, 28).

How many times do you have to hear it? How many times do you have to remind yourself who you really are? You are His daughter.

I met Patricia at Education Week when her husband, wearing a chartreuse aloha shirt, walked up to me and said, "Hi, I'm Mitch Huhem, and I want you to make my wife a queen!"

I didn't quite know what to say, but Patricia came for a personal workshop of several days with me in my home in San Francisco. Yes, I was her teacher for those few days, but it was my life that was blessed. We sat together, two sisters in the gospel of Jesus Christ, as she shared her unforgettable love story of God's guidance in bringing two people from different cultures together in a union to last the eternities. She has known depression, been overwhelmed, and she has suffered loneliness, poverty, and sorrow. She radiates the pure love of Christ, the true graciousness of

The Huhems

a queen, and compassion, much like that of Mother Teresa. Her story is shared here with her permission.

PATRICIA VILLARROEL HUHEM

I was born in northern Chile and served a full-time mission in the Chile Santiago South Mission. A year after returning from my mission, Elder Mitch Huhem was reassigned to serve in the Chile Antofagasta Mission to train leaders to become a stake. I was serving as the Young Women district president and attended his training. I was twenty-eight years old at the time and engaged to be married. In my career, I was the executive assistant to the mayor.

The day Elder Huhem was released from his mission I was attending the Santiago Chile Temple. I had just broken off my engagement and was trying to find peace. I wanted God to inspire me to know if I was to remain single. My university degree was in travel and tourism, so I thought maybe I needed to get a new job, go back to college, or travel. That night I went to the airport to say good-bye to a senior missionary couple. Elder Huhem was traveling on the same plane and, during the good-bye, a photo was taken of us shaking hands.

On Elder Huhem's flight home, he heard the still, small voice telling him, "Patricia is going to be your eternal companion." Mitch has since told me that the first time he heard the voice he thought, "This can't be. She's older; she's of a different culture, and she doesn't look like the type of girl I date." He heard the message three times in succession.

He began praying, fasting, and going to the temple. He didn't want to tell anyone of his promptings, not even his journal. He returned to school at BYU and went to the temple for guidance. He attended temple sessions and sealings. As he was kneeling across the altar, he tells me he heard my voice and saw my face. Immediately he wrote me a letter asking me about my plans in life, my testimony, and my impressions about family and children.

I thought that he might want to know more about my people and Chile. Someone had brought to my office the pictures of us shaking hands at the airport, so I replied and included the photo of us.

After Mitch received the letter, his mother asked who it was from.

Mitch showed her the photo, and she started to cry and said, "This is the kind of girl you are going to marry." When Mitch told her of his recent experiences, she suggested he call me.

When the phone rang, it was after midnight my time. My mother came to my bedroom and said, "Someone is on the telephone, but I cannot understand him."

"Hi, this is Elder Huhem. I need your fax number."

I gave it to him, and before we could say more, his mother grabbed the phone and started talking, but I couldn't understand English. Later he told me that she had said, "I'm so happy that you're going to be my daughter-in-law."

That night a three-page fax arrived. The first two pages explained the inspiration that he had received on the airplane. The last page had one question and two squares marked YES and YES.

It was so overwhelming that I was shaking. He called back to find out the answer. I said, "Elder Huhem, this is overwhelming, and if this is a joke, you picked the wrong person."

He answered, "No, this is the most serious thing I've ever done in my life."

"Then give me time to go to the temple."

I received a blessing from my father and the district president. In that blessing I was counseled to return to the temple, to fast and pray, and wait for answers to come.

Mitch kept calling me and asking what I was thinking. I always respected him. He wanted an answer, but I wasn't going to pretend.

A few weeks later I was reading the scriptures with my family and read 2 Nephi 4:23. "Behold, he hath heard my cry by day, and he hath given me knowledge by visions in the nighttime."

Heavenly Father had heard and answered my prayers. I knew Mitch was the right person for me. That night he called again! I told him my prayers had been answered, and I knew that he was the right person; however, my father had just been diagnosed with Alzheimer's and was in a mental clinic. I couldn't leave the country at that time.

We made a commitment to be engaged for one year. We would communicate by fax, cassette tapes, letters, and phone calls. I received my engagement ring with a cassette tape in the mail.

One year later, as Mitch arrived at the Santiago airport, I didn't know whether to call him Elder Huhem or Mitch. Our first date was to the Santiago Chile Temple. Since our government requires a civil marriage, we were first married in my home at 7 PM. We immediately got on the bus at 8:30 PM to ride thirteen hours to the temple. We arrived at 8 AM and were married in the temple two hours later.

We went on our honeymoon to the southern part of Chile. There the embassy informed us that the only way for me to be permitted to go to the United States would be for Mitch to return alone and then file a petition for me to follow a year later. Mitch traveled to the embassy every other week for the next two months, trying to find a way that I could go with him, but there were no exceptions. As Mitch's visa was to expire, he went to the embassy one last time to plead his case. They said, "No!"

We went outside to pray and decided to try one last time. Inside the embassy, a lady behind a desk said, "I am only allowed to grant an exception to your visa under 'the power of emergency' that could be applied to this situation. But you must leave the country within 24 hours." It worked. God had answered our prayers.

We had to leave from the embassy and go directly to the airport. It would have taken thirteen hours to return to my home. I called my parents from the embassy to say good-bye for the last time. On the airplane everyone was congratulating us as newlyweds, and I was sobbing because I was leaving my family, my homeland, and my people.

We arrived in Provo, Utah, before school started. Mitch was a seminary teacher and was starting a time management student planner. Things were financially rough for us. We were even sleeping on the floor.

We moved into student housing, and I got pregnant with our first baby. I would walk to my job at the temple laundry feeling depressed, homesick, friendless, and completely frustrated with the language. The first winter was unbearable. I had never even seen snow in my entire life. I called my bishop and told him, "I'm quitting. I'm leaving Mitch and going back home to my family."

He replied, "I know you're going to be awake tonight, so if by morning the Lord gives you approval, then go." I didn't get the approval.

My first baby, Adam Jared, was born. He lived only a short time. After we buried him, I was devastated. We knelt down together by the bed, sobbing. Mitch said, "We only have two choices: we can either rebel and blame God forever, or we can trust in Him no matter what." And that night, kneeling together, we gave our lives to the Lord.

Our second son, Moroni Brigham, was delivered by emergency C-section a year later. Within five weeks, Moroni passed away from heart failure. Yet another excruciatingly devastating time in our lives. We had lost our first two children, were penniless, but we still trusted the Lord.

We had patiently waited four years, and now the Lord had blessed us with a beautiful baby girl named Elisa. During the next four years we had three more wonderful children: Natasha, Christopher, and Camilla, who are all healthy and a great blessing to our lives.

As I look back over these years, I can say I have known poverty, depression, sorrow, frustration, loneliness, and being overwhelmed. I have felt the adversary trying to pull me down with discouragement, but through it all I have always known that I am a daughter of God who loves me and on whom I can depend forever.

Chapter 8

THE GIFT OF
REFINEMENT IN
APPEARANCE

B righam Young said, "Were you to see an angel, you would see a beautiful and lovely creature. Make yourselves like angels in goodness
and beauty" (*Discourses of Brigham Young,* 215).

Elder Douglas L. Callister, speaking at a Brigham Young University
devotional, said the following about the creations of our Heavenly Father:

"The nearer we get to God, the more easily our spirits are touched by
refined and beautiful things. If we could part the veil and observe our
heavenly home, we would be impressed with the cultivated minds and
hearts of those who so happily live there. I imagine that our heavenly parents are exquisitely refined. In this great gospel of emulation, one of the
purposes of our earthly probation is to become like them in every conceiv-
able way so that we may be comfortable in the presence of heavenly
parentage. . . .

"Brigham Young said: 'We are trying to be the image of those who live
in heaven; we are trying to pattern after them, to look like them, to walk
and talk like them.' . . .

The concept of refinement in appearance is one I speak on often. To me, being refined means having a polished appearance. So often we look into the mirror and don't like what we see anymore, yet we continue to do the same old things—use the same color of lipstick, blush, and eye shadows and wear the same old tired hairstyle. Sometimes, all we need to begin an inner transformation is to take a little time to make an outer transformation—to refine our appearance and elevate our confidence.

This chapter will stray a little bit from the purpose of the other chapters, but the tips here are sure to add a little glamour to your life and give you some ideas that will lead you on the path to physical refinement.

Let's begin!

SKIN CARE

Whether you are in your twenties or your eighties, it's crucial to care for your skin. As we age, the look of the skin becomes drab, wrinkled, and dry. Even younger skin needs help to stay beautiful. You do not need to buy expensive products. Cleanse your face night and morning with a non-drying cleanser. Never go to bed without cleansing your face and applying your night cream. Never use deodorizing bath soap for your face. Use soap designated specifically for the face. You can find a variety of inexpensive liquid facial cleansers at any drugstore. Purchase only those that are fragrance free.

Moisturizer. Make sure you use a good moisturizer to protect the skin. If your moisturizer does not contain sunscreen, be sure to add a layer of 45 SPF sunblock over the moisturizer. Note: Even the ultraviolet rays of indoor lighting can damage your skin.

Night Cream. Another by-product of aging is dry skin, especially if you live in a colder, drier climate. Purchase a special cream with more emollients to use for nighttime.

Facial Hair Removal. Most women find that after menopause facial hair becomes thicker and more apparent. Depilatories are special creams that remove facial hair easily and are available at any drugstore. It takes only about ten minutes, and the results are noticeably better. When you have superfluous hair, do not think that no one notices.

As I was babysitting my four-year-old granddaughter, her mother had told me that she liked to pretend to be an animal. I said, "Noël, why don't you pretend to be a bunny?"

She responded, "I can't, because bunnies have fur all over their faces. Grammy, you be the bunny. You have fur all over your face."

That was the day I started using a depilatory. Don't kid yourself that no one notices.

Skin Care Myths. Dr. Gary Friedman, a well-known plastic surgeon in San Francisco shared the following myths about skin care products:

- *Tissue and cellular extracts have anti-aging properties.* No way. This is false.
- *Collagen and elastin creams restore firmness and tone to the skin.* False too!
- *Aloe vera is a skin treatment wonder.* Again, this is false.
- *Royal bee jelly is an anti-aging agent.* Nope.
- *Cosmetics can cause tissue repair and cellular renewal.* Nope again.
- *Moisturizers can prevent wrinkles.* They don't.
- *Natural cosmetics are better.* Also false.
- *Astringents tighten the pores.* False.
- *Mineral oil and petrolatum, applied topically, clog pores.* False.

• *Cosmetics must be expensive to be effective.* Great news, this, too, is false.

So, there you have it. You don't need to buy into the ads you see on TV or the claims on that expensive product at the makeup counter; just do a few basic things, and your skin will look its best. And you'll save time and money too.

MAKEUP

Every woman has a basic knowledge of how to apply makeup, but here are some helpful ideas:

Use a Mirror. A magnifying mirror should be among your most important tools. Use one with 3x to 5x magnification. If makeup looks good close up, it will look even better from a distance. To tweeze eyebrows, use a 7x magnification mirror.

Foundation. Use a foundation that matches your skin tone. Be sure to test the color in the natural sunlight by putting a small amount along your jaw line. As we age and skin loses its elasticity and healthy glow, it is good to add some warm tones in your blushes and lipsticks. Ask at any major cosmetic counter in the larger department stores, and they will assist you with this. Foundation should never alter or add color to your skin. That is the function of blush and bronzers. Foundation is simply meant to enhance your natural skin tone. Dab foundation over your eyelids too. It cleans up tiny veins and uneven skin tones and acts as a primer for your eye shadows.

Powder. If desired, after foundation you can use powder for setting the foundation and for extending the wear of any other makeup products that will be applied. When powder is lightly dusted on with a brush, it will soften a look, eliminate shine, and keep foundation and eye shadows from creasing and forming lines around the eyes. Use a large, fluffy powder brush to apply powder. Note: Always brush in a downward direction. Brushing in an upward direction will make your hairs stand out, and you'll look like a bunny.

Blush. Begin your blush placement at the apple of the cheek. This is the fleshy area that plumps up when you smile. Make the color fade out in the direction of your temples. Start with a conservative amount. When searching for the most flattering blush hue, pinch your cheek—the right color will reveal itself. Reevaluate the color of your blush every few years. Skin tone changes over time, especially during and after menopause. As we age our skin many get ruddier, drier, or paler. You need to check that the tint of blush color you're wearing isn't an obvious strip across your cheek. Blush should make you look healthy. It should not be a splotch of color. Be sure to use a sponge or fluffy blush to blend and diffuse edges.

Eyelashes. Another fun tip that enhances the size and shape of your eyes is to curl your top lashes with an eyelash curler. Start curling at the base of your lashes, hold for five seconds, then move up a little, hold for five seconds, and look down while putting on your mascara. For more beautiful lashes, buy the mascara that has a primer at one end and mascara at the other. Use the primer first (sometimes called the conditioner), and then the mascara. And, on those days when a big makeup job isn't going to happen, remember that mascara, blush, and a quick application of lip color are three simple things you can put on before leaving the house.

Brows. Groomed and well-shaped brows provide a great final frame to the eyes. Use an eyebrow pencil that is close to the shade of your hair. It is important to use short hair-like strokes with your pencil. Blondes should choose a taupe-colored pencil. The main idea is to have brows look natural and not like you used a stencil. Be sure to pluck unwanted hairs in the direction that the hair grows. Use precision-slanted tweezers. I highly discourage the use of any permanent makeup. It will not only change colors, it will eventually be outdated.

Lip Color. Adding lip color is the simplest way to alter the way you look. When your lipstick fades after a few hours, it leaves you looking tired. Try the lip colors that last eight hours. They can be purchased at any drugstore. Make sure you have one lip color that blends with your skin tone and goes with everything. When you wear a strong lip color, like red, it's best to keep the rest of the face subdued. If your eyes are the focal point of your makeup, then use a more neutral lip color.

Choose one feature to be the focus. If you choose to have the mouth stand out, then have soft eyes (meaning less eye makeup). If you choose to have the eyes stand out, then have a soft mouth. If your lip color always seems to "travel," outline the lips with a pencil that closely matches the lip color before filling with the lip color. Lips are the pivotal point of the face. Beautiful lips can bring light and focus to your features and call attention to your smile.

About Hair

To help you on the hair front, I asked for some advice from one of San Francisco's leading color/stylists, Mark Schulte. Here are his suggestions—and a big reason to re-evaluate your hairstyle:

- A woman's hairstyle can have more influence on her self-esteem than almost any other aspect of her appearance. It truly is her crowning glory. If her hair looks good, she feels beautiful. And when

Before and after hair and make-up have been done.

she feels beautiful, the world looks better, which makes her life better.

- To find the right style for you, look in the mirror and be totally honest. What is your best feature? You need to create a look that puts focus on your best feature and draws attention away from less desirable features: beautiful eyes vs. a receding chin; full lips vs. no cheekbones. When you see a hairstyle on someone that you think would look good on you, take courage and ask the person who did their hair. Even a complete stranger will feel flattered. Then when you make your first appointment, ask for a consultation. This will give you some extra time when you are contemplating a major change. Even bring one or two pictures with you of hairstyles that you like.

- When the stylist is finishing your hair, be sure to ask questions about how to duplicate what he or she did. Also, ask about which products will be most beneficial to you. Which products thicken fine hair? Which products smooth and defrizz? Which shampoo will be best for your hair texture?

- Hairspray is sometimes a necessary evil. It dries out the hair and glues it together. But if you need it, try to find a spray that you can brush through and doesn't dull the hair. Hairspray that makes your hairstyle look like a helmet dates you back to the 60s; avoid it if that's the case!

- If you have thinning hair, it may be caused by a hormonal imbalance, thyroid problems, or a vitamin deficiency. It can also be caused by stress or even a medication you are currently taking. There are products available at any drugstore that are recommended by plastic surgeons and contain minoxidil, which has been proven to help thinning hair.

- Coloring your hair can literally transform you and take years off your appearance. Highlights are also a nice way to blend a few gray hairs and can give your hair a sun-kissed look. At first, you can cover gray with a semi-permanent color that lasts about six weeks. Later on, the semi-permanent color won't be strong enough, and you'll need to change to permanent dye. Dye will not ruin your hair. Dye can actually improve your hair and give it more body and shine.

  If you make the step to dye, you must be committed to taking care of the roots. You can do it yourself. Go to the hair color department in any drugstore and match their color swatches to your natural hair color. It's easy and inexpensive. Just be sure to follow the directions on the box.

- A few warm highlights in your hair, just as warm tones in your blush, can do wonders for the drab look that accompanies aging.

FASHION

The way you dress speaks volumes about who you are. Gratefully, that statement has nothing to do with the amount of money spent on clothing. It has to do with being well-groomed and having a polished appearance. I have been in countless classes at Education Week where the women model entire outfits purchased from Goodwill and garage sales or were presented as hand-me-downs. Their clothing is clean, pressed, complements their figure type, and is tastefully accessorized. Money is not the issue. My conclusions are that women don't take the time or want to do the planning that it takes to look their best except for special occasions. Following are items to help you look great every day:

Clean Your Closet. The first step to looking great is organize your closet so you can see what you have and what you need.

Remove everything unworn for a year, and put the clothes in a box to donate to Deseret Industries or Goodwill. Stop waiting to buy clothes until you've lost weight. Creating a refined and polished look starts right now.

Next, remove clothing that needs repair or alteration and put it where these repairs will get done.

Organize all your clothing in groups, putting similar items together—jackets, skirts, pants, tops, dresses, and so forth. If possible, line up your shoes and handbags so everything in your closet is in sight.

Make yourself a wardrobe list to post in your closet. The list will show all of the ways that you can mix and match what you have to make different outfits. With this list, if you see something at a garage sale you will know immediately if you have other pieces in your closet to wear with it. Buying some new, inexpensive accessories will update your old clothing.

Dress for Your Figure Type. Each of us has her own figure faults to work with. It's better to face the facts about your body proportions as they now exist and choose the clothes that will be most flattering. Why emphasize a figure fault when you can camouflage it? A garment that is too tight reveals body contours. Make sure that a new sweater isn't so tight that the lines of your bra are visible either in front or in back. Allow enough ease for smooth, unhampered motion; but don't allow your clothes to be so big that you look sloppy or so small that the garment looks skimpy. No matter what style you select in slacks or dresses, sit down in it before you buy it. Never purchase anything thinking you will someday lose weight and possibly fit into it.

Please be sure to look in a full-length mirror before leaving

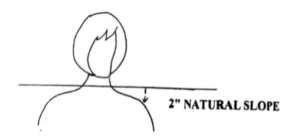

home. It is crucial to look at the back view. Make sure that your slip, underwear, or knee high hose does not show in the slit of your skirt.

Shoulder Pads. There are really only two reasons to ever wear shoulder pads: more than a two-inch natural slope (see note and illustration below) or narrow shoulders.

Note: Place a yardstick in the same position as the line in the above illustration. If you find that you have more than a two-inch natural slope, the addition of a small shoulder pad will definitely enhance your appearance.

COLOR

When you are wearing a flattering color, you will get compliments on how great you look or how rested you look. The right color can do wonders to brighten your eyes and even out your skin tone. The wrong color will have people telling you that you look tired and may draw attention to every flaw and wrinkle.

The colors that are best for you depend on your skin tone. A number of years ago the seasonal color theory was taught. Everyone had to fit into one of the four seasons of winter, summer, spring, and fall. The new and more updated trend, which has permeated most of the cosmetic companies, is to divide makeup into only two distinct palettes—one for cool undertoned women (formerly winter and summer), and one for warm undertoned women (formerly autumn and spring). This new trend in color gives more flexibility, especially when skin tones become drab due to aging. Some warm tones in hair and make-up will brighten drab skin in mature women. It may be helpful to go to one of the cosmetic counters in a large department store. Please note that there are many women that are considered "neutral," who can wear colors from both the cool and warm palettes.

Remember that colors come in many tones and hues. If olive green makes you look tired, chances are that emerald green will look wonderful on you, and so on.

The following chart provides examples of cool and warm tones.

Cool Tones	Warm Tones
Pure white	Off-white or cream
Burgundy red	Tomato/orangey red
Emerald green	Olive green
Powder pale yellow	Daffodil/lemon yellow

Which colors listed above look best on you? The cool tones or the warm tones? Note: Turquoise and coral look good on everyone. They are known as universal colors. Ultimately, you will find many wearable colors, compatible with your skin tone that you feel good about when you look in a mirror.

ACCESSORIES

Accessories are the finishing touch to every outfit. Learning to accessorize is an important step toward developing your own personal style. Today's best-dressed women always wear tastefully chosen accessories.

The main idea is to put together a perfect outfit by adding those extra accessories that complete a finished, polished look.

There are some people that never wear accessories, but you will find that if you add, for example, pearl earrings or a square neck scarf to even your jogging suit, you will have tied the bow on the package.

It's really simple to get accessory ideas. Just look in the fashion catalogs that come in the mail and not in the fashion magazines, which tend to be more trendy and overdone. Fashion catalogs show conservative accessories and are a good guide. If you do find something trendy that you like—go for it! However, if you are a more mature woman, please don't try to look like a teenager.

POSTURE

Good posture is important. Practice standing tall. Lengthen your neck, put your shoulders back, expand your chest, and tighten your stomach muscles. (Don't forget to breathe.) When you walk, think of yourself as lighter than air or think of walking on clouds. Do not walk "clunky," like a truck driver. Don't let your heel pound the ground first. Feel like you are walking as smoothly as if you were ice-skating.

SMILE

As you stand tall, smile, it's the best facelift you'll ever have.

Smile as you talk to people and make eye contact.

A smiling person is always judged as more pleasant, attractive, sincere, sociable, and competent than a non-smiling person.

Smiling releases endorphins that make us feel better.

Even 'faking' a smile can help us feel happier.

Some people may call this attention to the outward appearance vanity. But it certainly is not. Grooming ourselves out of a respect for others is a true compliment to them. Being careful to present ourselves well means that we think highly of those we are around, whether we are at church, at the workplace, or in our own homes.

I met Cindy at Education Week during one of my classes when she asked to come up on the stage. Along with changes to her hair and makeup, she told the audience that she had lost 100 pounds over the previous year. A desire to refine her appearance had prompted her to make the changes—and she did so with an insatiable desire to better herself.

Over time, I have come to know Cindy well. We have traveled together on speaking assignments, and she continues to amaze me. Her trials have been overwhelming. Hers is a story of courage, determination, and a willingness to serve Heavenly Father at any cost. I share it here with her permission.

CINDY WILSON'S STORY

I was an 11-pound, 12-ounce baby. I was obese at birth, and the doctor placed me on a diet at my first checkup. My mom said as a toddler I would go from table to table at restaurants and drink the little cups of cream sitting on the tabletops meant for coffee. I was obsessed with popcorn smothered in butter. I came from a family that is obese. I remember having banana splits for dinner sometimes.

I was 5'9" in the fifth grade and wore a size 11 shoe. The fifth grade was the year I started my first diet. I never thought the day would come that I could be a normal-sized person. In high school I was hooked on watching

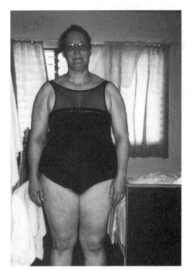

Cindy—before losing 100 lbs (the second time)

Cindy with her husband, Tom—after losing 100 lbs (the second time)

soap operas with my mom. I would race home from school, and sometimes we would each eat an entire cherry cheesecake while watching soap operas.

I started violin lessons in the fourth grade and have spent countless hours dedicated to my music. I was with the Spokane Junior Symphony and was the concert mistress in college.

I found the Church while attending college and while there I met my husband, Tom. We were best friends and had fun together. We fell in love, were married in the temple, and eventually had four children.

One of the most difficult trials I've had to endure in life was the loss of a child at birth. His name was Ross Thomas Wilson, Jr., and he lived only a few hours. I felt so hopeless. I was such a young mom, and I didn't know what to do. I just enjoyed my short time with my little baby, yet I remember feeling such a horrible loss.

I was emotionally and physically exhausted. As I arrived home from the hospital and opened my front door, I faced another disaster. I could *hardly believe my eyes. Our coal furnace had blown up, and black, buttery soot covered everything. There was no place to sit down without getting covered with soot, but I sat down and cried. Physically I was drained, but it forced me to have to do something when I didn't want to do anything. I had to get in and clean like I had never cleaned before.*

Shortly after that ordeal, we purchased a vintage farmhouse. On the way to church one Sunday, we stopped on the road to offer help to a homeless man. Little did I know that while we were at church, he would come into our home, build a fire in the center of our living room floor, and burn our house to the ground.

That same year we lost our corn crop in a fierce windstorm. Sometimes it seems that no matter how hard you work, things are rough. For me, these tragedies never seemed to stop.

When we finally paid off our house that had burned, a horrible flood came and wiped us out again. It was called a 100-year flood. It took livestock down the river and all the hay out of our barn. The Air National Guard took everyone's children by boat and helicopter to safety, and my husband and I stayed at the farm to try and save what we could. It was two weeks before we saw our children again. My family worked together to earn money to get us back on our feet. The children worked salvaging scrap metal to earn money, and to my family's credit, we were back on track before we knew it.

About this time, Barbara Barrington Jones came to our stake to give a women's conference. A story she told that day about a woman who changed her life inspired me to want to become my best self. I started by adding exercise into my daily life little by little. Eating foods in a natural state became my motto—no more gravies, sauces, and dressings. And sugar and fat were out.

I started improving my appearance by coloring the gray in my hair and wearing a little makeup. In one year I lost over 100 pounds. I finally had an opportunity to attend Education Week for the first time and thank Sister Jones, even though she didn't know me. Her words of encouragement helped me change the way I thought about myself. This change gave me the confidence to face the trials in my life.

Next, to my amazement, Barbara offered to help with a makeover. I went to a professional salon where they gave me a new hairstyle, applied my makeup, and even did my fingernails! I had always cut my own hair and permed it to a frizz, and I had never had my fingernails done. I sewed most of my family's clothes, so when Barbara asked me what I had brought to wear to have my photo taken, I was so proud of myself that I had bought a turquoise suit at Goodwill and had done a good job altering it to fit my slimmer body. Barbara taught me other important facets of refinement: manners, being gracious, writing thank-you notes, walking gracefully, and so on. I left truly feeling like a queen.

I was on the faculty of her women's program. I taught people how I had changed my mindset in order to be able to reach my weight goals. I had learned all of the refinements and the balance needed in my life, and I was taking care of my appearance. I had lost 100 pounds and kept it off for twelve years. It was also during these years that I taught seminary and gospel doctrine classes and studied the scriptures constantly.

When my two boys went on missions I somehow lost the balance that I had achieved when I lost my weight. I had to work three jobs to help pay for the missions and help my daughter's family a little financially, as she had just given birth to twins. It was the beginning of change back to a disastrous lifestyle.

I was so busy that I started eating treats—pizza, truffles, and ice cream. All of my old habits crept back. I stopped reading the scriptures on a regular basis as I had done when I taught seminary and gospel doctrine. There was just no time. I was too exhausted each night even to pray. I no longer cared about my appearance. I quit looking in the mirror, cutting my hair, putting on makeup, and exercising. I was depressed and unhappy. It was like being on a merry-go-round. I was up at 4:30 AM and fell into bed at 10:30 PM. I had now gained back all of the 100 lbs that I had lost, plus even more.

One night my depression became overwhelming. I felt as if I were going into a dark tunnel. I decided to take my life. My husband found me and took the gun from me that night. I'm very grateful for his intervention. I was diagnosed with clinical depression, and prescribed medication began to help.

When Barbara asked me to come back to help at her women's program, I was embarrassed about all the weight on me, yet everyone treated me with kindness. It helped me believe in myself because I knew if I had done it once that I could do it again. I felt like I needed to gain my confidence back, which I did.

I was able to once again change my mindset and put balance back into my life. I started taking care of my appearance. I was exercising, eating right, and drawing closer to the Savior to give me strength in facing a new diagnosis of multiple sclerosis. I needed Him now more than ever. And it was with His help that I once again lost another 100 pounds.

What I've learned from all of this is no matter what my challenges are in life, they're not going to change God's plan for me. I know that I am a daughter of God, and He knows and will help me through every trial. I know that I'm no different from you. I'm just a down-to-earth farm girl living on the same farm that I've lived on for thirty years.

Now I know the importance of the habit of reading the scriptures daily, of continuing to follow the Savior, and of personal prayer. I know I am a better representative of the Savior with my weight off. My greatest joy comes from serving others. I have a testimony of the gospel, and I know that the Savior lives and walks beside me and will give me His peace.

Chapter 9

THE GIFT OF HAPPINESS

Happiness doesn't just happen. Too many people spend their lives planning and hoping and dreaming about how wonderful their life would be if only. . . . We say we'll be happy when we lose thirty pounds or pay off our credit card debt. We act as if our happiness depends on other people, on fate, or on circumstances beyond our control. As a result, we fail to see how wonderful our lives are right now—today. When you continually look to the future for your happiness, you guarantee you'll never be happy.

I saw an article with a title that sounded like it could be a Dr. Seuss book, "Wherever You Are—Be There." To me that title says it all: don't live for the future; enjoy today. Psalm 118:24 says, "This is the day which the Lord hath made; we will rejoice and be glad in it."

How do you stop living only for the future? I believe the two most important steps are gratitude and finding balance in your life.

GRATITUDE

Gratitude is the first step toward a happier life. I'm sure there are things that you wish you had in your life. Even so, you still have many things for which to be grateful. Sarah Ban Breathnach, author of *Simple Abundance,* wrote "When we offer thanks to God or to another human being, gratitude gifts us with renewal, reflection, and reconnection. . . . [We ask, is] life abundant or is it lacking? . . . Once we accept that abundance and lack are parallel realities and that each day we choose . . . which world we will inhabit, a deep inner shift in our reality occurs. We discover the sacred in the ordinary and we realize that every day is literally a gift. . . . how we celebrate it, cherish it and consecrate it is how we express our thankfulness to the Giver of all good" (*Simple Abundance: Living by Your Own Lights,* 1996).

The choice Ban Breathnach encourages us to make is captured in a well-worn cliché: Is the glass half empty or half full?

There is power in gratitude. Gratitude truly gifts the giver. Alma 34:38 says, "Humble yourselves even to the dust, and worship God, in whatsoever place ye may be in, in spirit and in truth; and that ye live in thanksgiving daily, for the many mercies and blessings which he doth bestow upon you."

Sister Marjorie Pay Hinckley said, "'Thank you' is a wonderful phrase. Use it. It will add stature to your soul. Never let a day go by without saying thank you to someone for something—and especially to your Heavenly Father" (*Glimpses into the Life and Heart of Marjorie Pay Hinckley,* 91).

During a recent tour of South Africa, I visited a squatters' camp outside of Johannesburg. The houses there are made of corrugated tin and lined with cardboard. The tin roofs are low and weighted down with rocks to prevent the windstorms from blowing them away. The ladies carry heavy bundles and baskets on their heads.

I saw a five-year-old boy playing by himself and I asked, "Hi, what are you doing?"

He said, "This is the best day."

"Why?" I asked.

"Because I'm playing with this grasshopper. I'm making marks for him, and he does races and I'm having so much fun." He had been playing with a grasshopper and a stick.

I thought to myself, "This boy lives in poverty, but he is happy." Then I thought about the discontent, the wants, and the whining of many of the children in America who have everything and take it all for granted.

As we drove to another squatters' camp up on a hill overlooking a breathtaking view of the ocean, I turned around and I saw a fence with thirty preschoolers and one woman standing behind it. The branch president told me that only one woman takes care of all of the children and even prepares a hot bowl of corn meal mush daily. The mothers who leave their children there while they work pay 60 rand a month, or 10 US dollars. The lady in charge is never able to make ends meet, but she does it because of the children.

When I looked at all these precious little children, with their runny noses and smudged faces, I could see that they were happy. They had no toys, no books, nothing, but they were happy with life and thrilled to have visitors. They were grateful for just being there. They put their arms around our legs, jabbering with excitement. Then the teacher asked them to sing us a song. They started singing a cute African song, doing movements with their hands as they sang. I was so grateful to be there with them.

Teaching Gratitude. After the suicide death of my first husband and my new marriage to my husband, Hal Jones, I realized that one of the most important values I needed to teach my children was gratitude for a new dad who loved them and would care for them. I worked hard when I remarried to show my husband how grateful I was to him for taking on my two children. Hal was twenty-six years older than I, and he had already raised his family. My little girl, Wendy, was in the first grade and my son, John, was in the fifth. I wanted so much for them to be grateful to this man who was their new father. He tried so hard to be patient. I had them make thank-you notes to him for everything. They soon began to call him Dad. He was a wonderful father. We were married twenty-seven years before he passed away. He helped with birthday parties, went to soccer games and ballet recitals, and once even helped Wendy make a dove costume for the Christmas play.

Wendy hugs dad before leaving for her misison in Honduras.

When Wendy was in the first grade she came home from school and asked, "Dad, I'm going to be a dove in the Christmas play. Will you make me a costume?"

I overheard the conversation, thinking to myself, "He's a heavy construction person, not a costume designer." But he wanted to be a good dad. He said, "Okay, get a pillowcase, a magic marker, and some scissors."

She brought him everything he requested. He said, "We'll cut a hole for

your head, one for each arm and write on the pillowcase, 'I am a dove.'"
He truly tried his hardest, and, believe it or not, Wendy was thrilled!

Before my husband passed away, my daughter told me that one day
she heard a song on the radio that she had never heard before. The song
brought her to tears, and she suddenly realized, "I owe so much to Dad."
He had raised her, been there when she was sealed to her eternal companion in the temple, and had held her two children in his arms. Inspired
by the song, she had an overwhelming urge to sit down and write him a
letter. She thanked him for making her dove costume in first grade. "Dad,
I'm so grateful that you talked me into going on a mission, for being there
when I took out my endowments, when I was married and sealed in the
temple, and for being there to hold your grandchildren."

Her letter thanked him for everything and told him about the song
that she had heard. "Dad, the message of this song told exactly how I feel
about you. It spoke of thinking back on all of the wonderful times we have
had together, and of the memories and dreams that are now a part of the
past. However, the words that made me cry were, 'I am so grateful that I
was blessed to have you in my life.' Thank you for always being there for
me. You were my strength, my wisdom, and my reason for trying to reach
the stars. I owe so much to you. You will forever have a special place in
my heart. I love you, Dad."

When Hal finished reading the letter, the tears were streaming down
his cheeks. He handed the letter to me, and as I read it through my tears,
I thanked God for helping me to teach my daughter gratitude, gratitude
for this incredible man that loved her with all his heart. Hal passed away
only a few months after Wendy had been inspired to write her letter.

My son, John, was a good boy. He had been with me through some of
the saddest and most arduous times in my life. It was harder for him to

have a new dad, because he was older than Wendy and had vivid memories of his natural father.

I remember one funny incident when I had just married Hal and we
had moved to San Francisco. John was in the fifth grade. He and Wendy
were students at a Catholic school. He came home from school one day
quite wide-eyed. "Mom, you'll never believe this! Today in religion class,
we learned The Lord's Prayer! It goes like this! 'Our Father which art in
heaven, Hal will be thy name!'" I couldn't wait until Hal got home that
evening to tell him the story. "Well, you've got it made now, John thinks
you're God."

John was not an easy boy for Hal to raise. All he wanted to do was
read, listen to music, and 'hang out' with his friends. Hal, however, coming from a background of poverty and hard physical labor, wanted to teach
John his work ethic and how to be a real man. It was sometimes a rocky
road, but on Hal's seventy-fifth birthday, John wrote a tribute to his dad:

"On Being a Man."

"The recurring theme of my relationship with my father could be
entitled 'On Being a Man.' And if you know my father, you know that the
word *recurring* is a drastic understatement. When I was age eight, he
came into my life and until this very day, much of his talk has centered on
being a man—what it means, what a man does, etc.

"As a child, it simply passed through me. But as I reached my teens it
began to carry more worth. I was forced to ponder the question. What
does it mean to be a man?

"The media's portrayal of it all served to confuse me even more. Did
it mean sweating more? Did it mean holding your liquor? Losing your vir-
ginity? Did it mean working out and drinking Gatorade? Frankly, it all

scared me. Here I was, being pulled from all sides into 'becoming a man,' and not really feeling comfortable with it.

"Faced with the choice of many different paths all purporting to lead to manhood, in the end, I chose my father's, the Hal Jones path. Not that I knew what it meant. I honestly never knew. Why did I have to work in the yard every Saturday? Why couldn't I have a Dad-illac (a car given to you by your parents) like everyone else? Why couldn't I sleep in till noon on Saturdays? Why did I have to participate in this and that when I'd much rather be in my room reading a book? I never knew, and I murmured much during those high school years. But underneath it all, I trusted my father. Whenever I doubted, I could always look to him, and how he has lived and who he has become, and renew my commitment to stay on 'his' path. But I still didn't know, even after my mission.

"Then, last year, the storms came. My life was suddenly flooded with painful trials and tough times, the kind of which I had never experienced before. Things could not possibly get any worse, I would say, and then they would. So often I felt like I was in way over my head, treading water, and in danger of drowning or getting sucked under.

"I turned to my God, and instinctively, almost without realizing it, I turned to the man that lay inside me, dormant, the result of years of learning and experience, the man that my father had shaped and molded.

"The storms have now passed, and as I come up for air, I look back and am amazed at the fortitude I possess. How did I weather it all so well? The answer came in a flash, as those life-affirming answers always do, and I realized I had stayed on the path and become that man that my dad had talked about for so long.

"And what does it mean to be a man to me now? It means strength and self-confidence through being centered on Christ, and being able to

John Jones graduates from PSU.

work hard and enjoy it. It means giving more than you take. It means responsibility, keeping agreements, finishing what you start, and doing what you say you will do. It means perseverance. When you fall down in life, you need to get up. It means discipline, doing what you do not want to do to accomplish what you want to accomplish.

"Dad, I am who I am today because of you. Thank you so much. I love you."

One year after my husband passed away, John graduated from Portland State University. It had been a long and hard road for John, with many trials and interruptions. After the graduation ceremony, dressed in his cap and gown, John walked up to me, placed a thin green satin stole around my neck with the PSU logo on the bottom and handed me a card. In John's beautiful printing was written,

"As the earthly representative of my father, who has passed away, I present this 'stole of gratitude' to you to thank my dad for always believing in me, and supporting me in getting my education. I would have never made it to this day without him. Thank you, Mom. Love, John."

I am grateful to Heavenly Father for helping me to teach my children gratitude.

FINDING BALANCE IN LIFE

The second step to a happier life is finding the balance—or harmony—in life. When life becomes unbalanced, depression follows, and depression among women is of epidemic proportions in today's world. There are four facets of life that must be balanced in order to live life to its potential. Those facets are: your brain, your physical body, your spiritual self, and your social/emotional self.

For twenty-nine years, Hal was my role model for living a balanced life and taking care of himself. He exercised not just his body, but his mind, his spirit, and his generosity towards others. In his masculine way he would say, "If you don't use it, you'll lose it." I will never be able to be as disciplined as he was, but I gained a tremendous amount of knowledge from him. As you read his philosophy, I hope that you will be challenged to try to put more balance in your life. Depression begins to flee when gratitude and balance begin to take over your life.

Exercise Your Brain. Exercise your brain by reading good literature and by continuing to study and learn. After Hal had partially retired, he instituted a daily study time. He read the *Ensign,* business books, self-help books, and even detective novels. I am not the avid reader that my husband was, but I do believe that the person who doesn't read is no better than the person who can't read. I have a note on my mirror that says, "R.E.D."—read every day!

Exercise Your Physical Bodies. Hal believed in daily walking and daily exercises to strengthen the upper body. He walked about forty-five minutes to an hour daily. In his younger years he played handball five days a week, but even on the last day of his life, at age eighty-six, he finished his walking routine through the house before he sat down on the edge of the bed and was gone in an instant. He was able to retain that physical discipline to the last day of his life. Since I was a former classical ballet dancer, I, too, have always exercised and stretched daily, but Hal truly was my role model for consistency.

Eat nutritious food. My husband wanted to eat simple, basic foods—the way that God made them. Before he was a member of the Church, he was living the Word of Wisdom and didn't know it. He ate lots of fresh fish, rarely ate red meat, and frequently ate oatmeal, bran cereal, fresh vegetables, salads, fruit, cottage cheese, and so on. He loved any kind of sugar-free dessert that I would make. He also loved chocolate, but he rarely ever indulged. I know it sounds boring, but since I cooked all of the meals for all those years, I learned to enjoy his nutritious ways of eating. Now that I live alone, my eating habits are not as disciplined, and I can tell you that when I ate the more nutritious way, I felt better.

Exercise Your Spirit. My husband had the most humble prayers. He knelt by his bed each night and prayed to Heavenly Father for the longest time before he retired. When I asked him why it took him so long, he said that it was because he had so much to be grateful for. He read the scriptures daily and studied Church magazines and books, biographies of the prophets and Apostles, and so on. At the urging of one of his doctors, Hal kept a journal of letters for the last fifteen years of his life. His doctor encouraged him to write letters to himself as if he were his own best friend. (I have all these letters now, and they have sentences like, "Hal you're such a lucky guy. You have a wife who loves you, work that you love, and a church that has blessed your life and your family's lives.") I realized that those letters were a beautiful way to count your blessings, and to pen your gratitude for God, family, life, and nature. Looking at life through the prospective of your best friend allows you to see just how truly blessed you are.

Exercise Your Spirit, by Giving. The fourth aspect of balance is giving of yourself, which strengthens your spirit. My husband was blessed in that aspect. At his funeral, two men who had never met started talking. The one man of Latin descent said, "Hal helped my son on his mission." The other man, one of Hal's relatives, said, "When my daughter was young he helped with her surgery for scoliosis, and she has walked tall all her life." The janitor of Hal's company said that Hal had helped his daughter go to college, and one of the workmen remembered a time when the company hadn't made enough profit to pay any bonuses. Hal went down to the bank and borrowed the money so his employees would still get a bonus. The list could go on for countless pages. He always told me, "Never go to bed unless you have given more than you have taken!" For me, this philosophy of giving has changed my life forever. My goal is to continue Hal's "Legacy of Giving," and hopefully teach it to my grandchildren.

LEARN HOW TO STEP BACK FROM LIFE

I'm sure you've heard it said that time is money. Well, time isn't just money; it's happiness! Georgia Witkin, Ph.D., and author of *The Female Stress Syndrome Survival Guide*, writes, "The time deficit women feel is the number-one daily happiness drainer. . . . It's not a matter of poor time management, because women are amazingly efficient. The problem is that we tend to overextend ourselves and try to take care of everyone else first." (qtd. in Corbett, "Be Your Happiest Self: Easy Ways to Take Charge of Your Life Right Now," 78). That is part of our nurturing nature.

With this in mind, I'd like you to, in the midst of your chaotic daily schedule, pause, step back from life, and take a breath. In a study conducted by Harvard University, scientists came to the conclusion that pausing for five minutes, four times a day, can cut your stress level in half. Dr. Witkin says, "It reminds your body what it feels like not to be on adrenalin overload" (qtd. in Corbett, "Be Your Happiest Self: Easy Ways to take Charge of Your Life Right Now," 78). You will think more clearly, you will get more accomplished, and you will stop getting so easily sidetracked. Sometimes we race through our day, getting sidetracked from the tasks that were on our list in the morning, and by bedtime, completely exhausted, we wonder what was accomplished? Stop, for just five minutes, breathe, refocus, and connect with your divine center.

Each day, try to take one thing off your to-do list to give yourself a pause. The difficult task with downtime, which you have now achieved for yourself, is to just do nothing. Your tendency will be to fill it with another task. Try taking a longer shower or sitting and enjoying the sunset. But your greatest blessings of peace and tranquility will come from learning to see God in nature. In nature you can see the harmony in the universe and in the seasons. You will experience a special closeness to God that cannot be felt in any other way.

Twenty-five years ago, my husband and I committed to memory a prayer that we recited together every morning. "For the beauty of the earth, For the beauty of the skies, For the love which from our birth Over and around us lies, Lord of all, to thee we raise This our hymn of grateful praise" (*Hymns*, no. 92).

If you feel yourself getting ultra-critical of things, or if you find yourself no longer marveling at the wonders in life, step back from what you are doing. You may be pressing too hard. Lie down on your back in an open field and gaze at the vastness above.

Frederick M. Lehman, in his beautiful hymn "The Love of God," wrote, "Were every stalk on earth a quill, And every man a scribe by trade; To write the love of God above Would drain the ocean dry" (in *Evening Light Songs*, 484). Thank God for all the good, all the beauty, and all the love He has put into your life. Chances are you are way ahead of the game. For eyes to see golden sunsets, for ears to hear meadowlarks sing, for tongues to taste just-picked raspberries, and for a million other things, we thank you, dear God.

One day, years ago, my visiting teaching companion asked me to accompany her to the home of a young mother who had been brutally attacked, bludgeoned with a club, and left for dead. Her name was Betsy. Betsy had been in the hospital for weeks and had just been sent home. The Relief Society sisters were there in teams to help with children, the cooking, the cleaning, and so on. Every bone in sweet Betsy's face had been broken, and her jaw had to be wired shut. The sisters had to be prepared to use special wire cutters in case she started choking. I remember hearing shocking details of her frightening attack.

As I sat in the living room, I saw the photo of a slim, young woman in a runner's outfit with a number on the front. I learned that the picture was of Betsy; and I couldn't imagine how such a small woman had survived. I can testify to you without a shadow of a doubt, that the woman who emerged from that tragic attack was transformed that day into an angel of our Heavenly Father, sent here to bless the lives of each person she meets. She is truly a role model for the "Gift of Happiness." I reprint Betsy's story here with her permission.

Betsy before her accident

BETSY BOREN'S STORY

My parents divorced when I was a small child, at which time my mother was institutionalized, leaving just me and my dad. He was a truck driver. He went to my kindergarten teacher and asked, "Do you have any ideas of where I could leave Betsy while I'm out of town?" She suggested my friend Carolyn's house. My dad asked her parents if I could stay there, and I did.

When my dad came to pick me up, I hid under the dining room table. They told him that I could stay if he wanted to leave me because they had always wanted more children. I stayed for eighteen years. My dad moved to Washington D.C., and I never really heard from him again.

I met my husband, Terry, as a freshman in high school. We dated at the end of high school. I attended Santa Rosa Junior College, and Terry would come home from BYU and visit. Terry baptized me while I was in college and then we were married.

Turning the clock ahead to that fateful day. We had become a family of four at this time, and our daughters were ages fifteen and eleven. We lived in a wonderful neighborhood. It was August, and we had just returned from a two-week vacation with my in-laws. I was a runner, and once we got home, I was anxious to start running to lose those extra vacation pounds.

On Monday I set out from home. As I was running, I actually passed the man that would attack me. He was a huge, black man wearing only trunks. I noticed the V-shape of his immensely defined muscular back. I noted all of this while I was running and while he was walking and dragging a large branch along the side of the building. "This man does not belong here. He is out of place." It flashed through my mind that I should not run on my usual isolated path.

I had never run around a track in my life, but he was behind me, and I didn't want him to see me going down the isolated path. I decided to run my entire five miles around the school track. I finished my run and went home.

It was Monday night. We all ate dinner outside. I told my husband about the incident, but he didn't give it much credence, and it really bothered me.

On Wednesday I entered my same open path by the creek to our school. Then . . . I don't remember anything. I have a gigantic black hole in my life. I have even gone back to that place many times trying to remember, but as hard as I try I cannot remember anything. People say it's God's way of protecting me. I remember waking up in the hospital in pain. I recognized my husband, and I thought I had children on the other side of the wall. I didn't know how to get to them, but I knew they were all right.

"What had happened to me?" My husband told me that as he was driving home he passed the street where the attack happened. He saw sheriff cars, helicopters, and commotion everywhere and wondered what was going on. Apparently the attacker had lain in wait for me. Since Terry was an assistant district attorney he couldn't help but know something serious had happened.

He saw the soccer coach, Jim, who told him a woman was walking her dog and heard someone moaning in the creek. Jim found the woman left in the water for dead, beaten beyond recognition, and called for help. (Jim knew me but didn't recognize me because every bone in my face was broken.)

Terry asked a deputy sheriff what had happened, and he asked Terry if I had gone running today.

Terry said, "Probably."

"What color shoes did she have on?"

Terry replied, "Salmon."

"You better come with me to the hospital."

Even my own husband didn't recognize me. My head was the size of a watermelon. Of course, there were too many other problems to even begin to mention.

As I lay in the hospital for weeks, my husband would come to my bedside. He was the only person I recognized. I would beg him to untie me. I had tubes everywhere. "Please untie me; I feel like a prisoner." My hands were tied to the post of the bed. My children didn't get to see me for weeks. My husband would ask me questions to test my memory, and I hated it. What town do you live in or what street do you live on? I would always answer Pizza Town and Pizza Street because my mouth was wired shut, and all I knew was that I was hungry.

The doctors told Terry that I should be institutionalized. I could never be left alone. Our ward had a fast for me. Terry took me home, and the Relief Society organized teams of sisters to stay with me the first month.

I've had many surgeries since then. I had to have a new nose and cheek implants to give me a new face. I have had extensive physical therapy for my balance, and one of the most difficult realizations for me to accept was that with my balance and depth perception problems, I would never be a runner again. As a runner I had finally conquered my weight problem. I felt discouraged that I would never have a runner's body again.

It's been over two decades since the attack happened, and I still have effects every day mentally. I forget things easily. The other thing is that I forget all the time. See, I forgot that I already wrote that. My life will never be what it was before. I have lost the use of parts of my cognitive skills, and my mental capacity is permanently impaired.

The sheriff had a helicopter out looking for the man who had attacked me. They finally caught him. He was sentenced and convicted.

So, what were the blessings from this life-altering event? Gratitude! Gratitude for life! Gratitude for each and every day that I can be with my family. Gratitude for the realization that I had chosen the very best husband in the entire world!

My visiting teaching companion asked me why I'm not bitter. I answered, "I'm too busy getting back my life and into the lives of my husband and children to waste energy and time being bitter." I was grateful that my daughters got to be closer to their dad. He was forced to be a mom and a dad. He had never been into the details of their lives before. He was always at work. They came to rely on him, and I can see the blessings of that even now.

Terry also started teaching early morning seminary for our girls' benefit and then became the bishop.

Each day is precious to me. I would think to myself, "What if I hadn't survived?" I would never have been able to see my girls growing up. I treasure the memories of little insignificant experiences with my girls that I'm sure most people would have taken for granted.

There is also the inexpressible joy and gratitude of being a grandmother of five. It's surprising how much you can love them. I love being a grandmother because at this stage we grandmas can overlook the little quirks and not worry so much.

I love nature, to be able to see, experience, and feel God's love in the beauty that is surrounding me. This summer all eleven of our family went together to Red Fish Lake in Idaho. We rented a big motorboat and drove to the center of the lake. I just sat there basking in this unforgettable moment with my husband, my daughters and their spouses, and my five precious grandchildren. I looked up at the majesty of those massive mountains, the clear blue sky, and the serenity of the lake; I breathed in the scent of pine trees in the cool mountain air. I said to myself, "This must be just like the celestial room in heaven. The happiness I feel today is His ultimate gift to me."

Betsy Boren, far right, with all her family at Red Fish Lake in Idaho

Chapter 10

THE GIFT OF TRUST

Abeautiful scripture that has made an impact in my life is Psalms 139:9–10: "'If I take the wings of the morning, and dwell in the uttermost parts of the sea; Even there shall thy hand lead me, and thy right hand shall hold me." This scripture speaks to me, saying that no matter where my life may take me—"on the wings of the morning"—I will never be alone. He will always go before me, leading me and holding me with his right hand. I can say with complete and unshakable confidence, "Father I trust in Thee!"

Over the past twenty years, I have had a number of experiences that came about at times when I could not see what was in the future but had to rely on the Lord, to let His plan for my life be revealed. To trust Him. This chapter is the story of my path, and the lessons I learned by trusting in Him.

GO IN PEACE

After speaking for the Church for about ten years, I found in my mailbox a letter inviting me to Australia. "Australia, hurray!" I was excited to go, and plans were falling into place when my doctor found two large tumors on my ovaries. At the same time, my Aunt Jane had been diagnosed with tumors on her ovaries, and the biopsy had shown they were malignant. My aunt's doctor faxed my doctor the report that stated, "Please get Barbara to surgery immediately."

My doctor said, "You read this fax. What are you going to do?"

I thought to myself, "'If I take the wings of morning'... even there will He be with me."

So I said to my doctor, "What would you think if I went?" I told him that I felt God wanted me to go to Australia.

My doctor responded, "I'm with you. I have a good feeling about this, and we will do the surgery immediately upon your return."

The day I left, I received a note from my dad's neighbor, Cloteal. She is ninety years old, an extremely spiritual woman, and seemed to always have inspiration regarding my life. She wrote, "I found this scripture for you, and I know it is for your trip, 'Go in peace, the mission you are on is under the eye of the Lord,'" (a paraphrase from Judges 18:6).

Australia was unforgettable. I met wonderful people and heard inspirational stories. It was the trip of a lifetime that I will never forget.

INTO SURGERY

I returned and immediately went to the hospital for the surgery. I was afraid and told Heavenly Father, "the outcome is in thy hands and the rest doesn't matter." He had given me so much. I was willing to face whatever I needed to go through. Since my aunt's tumors had been cancerous, I prepared myself for the worst.

The surgery went well; the tumors were benign. I remember that night after Hal left the hospital. I bowed my head and into my mind came this scripture, "He that sent me is with me: the Father hath not left me alone" (John 8:29). He once again had led me on the wings of the morning.

I felt His closeness to me and whispered, "Heavenly Father, thank you."

I felt the still small voice reply, "You have much work to do." The tears streamed down my cheeks. Even though I have more work to do, my life's mission will not make me exempt from trials. I must continue to trust and say, "Not my will, but thine." I know that I will never have to be alone. "The Lord is my shepherd; I shall not want" (Psalm 23:1).

A Two-Year Lawsuit Unfolds

Three months after Hal's death in 2003, I found myself embroiled in a lawsuit that questioned my husband's competence at the time he wrote his will. With this lawsuit came the possibility of me losing everything, even our home. It was one of the most stressful events of my entire life because it was compounded by grief.

One night when I was in the thick darkness of this lawsuit, I turned on BYU-TV, and Sheri Dew was speaking. During her talk she said that she was currently facing one of the greatest trials of her life. (She did not elaborate.) She said that she had pleaded with the Lord for an answer. She had fasted, increased her temple attendance, but, still, there was no answer. Then in the midst of this storm, she said that she asked herself, "So, Sheri, do you believe in God? Of course I do. And do you believe that He will help you? Of course I do."

Then I started to cry. Heavenly Father was saying to me through her words, "Barbara, do you believe in me?" Of course I do. "And do you believe that I will help you?" Of course I do. "Then trust me."

I attended the temple, kept a list of scriptures that helped me, and prayed my way through each day. I added to this scripture list often. I kept one by my bed, one in my purse, and another on my bathroom mirror. The list started with Proverbs 3:5, "Trust in the Lord with all thine heart; and lean not unto thine own understanding."

One year later the lawsuit had escalated. I found that my time was being completely consumed reading countless legal documents, going through hospital records, and attending depositions.

One day my attorney called to ask me to come to his office for some good news. When I arrived he was elated to tell me that we had been given a trial date of April 15. At that time some type of decision would finally be reached. He felt confident that we would win, but in a court of law, there are no guarantees.

I gulped as I heard the date. Almost six months prior to this conversation, the Public Affairs Committee of the Church in South Africa had invited me to do a five-week speaking tour beginning March 30 and ending May 6. I timidly explained this to my attorney.

In an uncomprehending and firm manner he said, "Do you realize how important this trial date is? This trial will determine your future. And I know that your church doesn't even pay you! What could you be thinking? It will take us months to get a new trial date."

I said, "Well, I'll have to give you my decision tomorrow. I need to ask."

Since I live alone, he retorted, "And whom are you going to ask?"

I firmly said, "God!"

He said, "God? You're going to ask God?"

I resounded with, "That's right!"

The next day I returned to his office with a big smile on my face. My attorney took one look at me and said, "I know, I know, God said yes, you are supposed to go." I didn't really need to answer my attorney. He already knew. (And he was right. We couldn't get another trial date for five months.)

I trusted Heavenly Father, knowing that I was on the Lord's errand and that He would take care of everything if I would but diligently serve Him. One day as I was outside walking and listening to a tape of general conference, I heard President Gordon B. Hinckley use a scripture so powerful that I began to cry. He quoted from Joshua 1:9: "Be strong and of a good courage; be not afraid, neither be thou dismayed: for the Lord thy God is with thee whithersoever thou goest." I knew that I would be directed in God's path. I looked back over the previous twenty years of my life, and I wondered how I would have ever guessed that I would have had the opportunity to serve Him in Guatemala, El Salvador, Mexico, Hawaii, New Zealand, Canada, Australia, England, and now South Africa.

Into Africa

The mission of the Public Affairs Committee of South Africa is to bring the Church out of obscurity. My itinerary showed seventy-five different speaking venues in a five-week period. It was the most frightening schedule I have ever faced. I would be speaking mainly in the public arena: to 10,000 teenage girls in nineteen private schools; to six colleges and universities; to chambers of commerce; to Rotary clubs; to the Women's Christian Democratic Party; to insurance companies; and even to a reformatory. There were thirty venues in addition to Church firesides and meetings with missionaries.

It was the most exhausting, exhilarating, spiritually humbling trip of my life. I not only left San Francisco trusting that Heavenly Father knew what I had to leave behind, but also with trust in the unknown in South Africa. I faced a schedule that seemed humanly impossible.

The schedule was also too tight for any preparation time. For the first time in my life as a speaker, I had to simply rely on Heavenly Father to give me the right words during each and every talk. I so clearly remembered that September day nearly thirty years before when the Lord had spoken to me through the scripture telling me, "The Lord God hath given me the tongue of the learned, that I should know how to speak a word in season to him that is weary: he wakeneth morning by morning, he wakeneth mine ear to hear as the learned" (Isaiah 50:4).

THE REFORMATORY

One particular day in Africa stands out as most memorable. I found myself in the Norman House Reformatory, a safe house for troubled youth, sometimes known as Lost Children. They had been rejected by their parents, and society had no place for them to go except to a prison-like facility. Many had been involved in serious crimes—hijacking, robbery, drug abuse, and stealing so their families could eat. Some of them had AIDS, and most of them could not read or write.

It was an unforgettable experience. As I stood in front of the group to begin my talk, they were rowdy, disruptive, shoving, talking, and generally not paying attention. Others just stared at me. Even though I'd been told not to bother with American humor because they wouldn't understand it, I knew that the only way I could get their attention was to make them laugh. With some trepidation, I decided to pull out my comedy character, Melweena.

I told them a joke that I had tested on our safari guide. It worked! They started to laugh. That was just what I had hoped for. I told them joke after joke, and they were now laughing and having fun. Finally, I told them the story of my life, my discouragement, my low self-esteem, my years of abuse and the times I was held at gunpoint. I told them of the years of living in fear and wishing that I were dead. In some ways, I had been where they were, not in a real prison, but in a lonely prison without walls.

By the end of my allotted time, they were leaning forward, holding hands, listening. They begged us all not to leave and asked all of us to sign autographs because hardly anyone ever came to visit them. All the members of the Public Affairs Committee were so grateful that they had come along with us. At that moment and at many other times in Africa, I was so grateful Heavenly Father had given me the right words to speak.

Following our trip to the Norman House, our Public Affairs representative took us to the University of Johannesburg where I spoke to the Golden Key Honor Society. These intellectual college students came in wondering what this speaker from America would tell them. I knew that Heavenly Father wanted me to begin by telling them my story of adversity and abuse. With so much abuse in Africa, they could certainly relate to my story. Then I would trust Him to guide me with the rest.

After telling a shortened version of my story, I said these words, "I want to tell you the story of my husband's life." I thought, "Where did that sentence come from? I never tell Hal's story."

My wonderful husband Hal was born in poverty in Iowa. His father declared bankruptcy when Hal was about six. They moved to Oakland, California, when he was seven. He began selling watered-down lemonade in the stands at the stadium during the baseball games at the age of ten. At fourteen, he had added two paper routes to his jobs and saved every penny. At this young age, his early goal was to never be poor again.

Hal saved enough to purchase a cement mixer. He made square stepping stones. His profit was 15 cents for each stone he made. He put himself through the University of California at Berkeley and continued to take night classes even after receiving his degree. He never stopped learning. At the end of his life, he had created and owned thirteen companies in the San Francisco Bay area with hundreds of employees. These companies built roads and bridges and sold sand, gravel, concrete, and asphalt. He was a self-made man who lived his own formula for success, a formula of self-mastery. He felt that anyone using this formula could reach their potential. He would say: You must have balance in your life, as you strive to better yourself in these six crucial areas: (1) mental—always continue to learn; (2) physical—eat right and exercise everyday; (3) spiritual—keep the lines of communication between you and God open; (4) social/emotional—never go to bed having taken more than you've given to your fellow man; (5) self discipline—Hal's mother taught him, "Life is like a cable, you weave a strand a day of good habits or of bad habits;" (6) attitude—A positive attitude will color your life in stunning ways. Keep a smile on your face and good thoughts in your mind. You must have this balance in your life to be a success.

I told this group that they needed to practice this formula of self-mastery. Each one couldn't rely only on intellect alone, because no matter how smart you are, you must have balance. And most important, you need to give of yourself. If you do not give of yourself, you will never find success, happiness, and fulfillment in this life.

At that moment, I looked down at my sheaf of papers on the podium and saw the name and phone number of the Norman House Reformatory. I felt the Spirit urging me so strongly to give this group the phone number.

I turned around and wrote the number on the board behind me as prompted by the Spirit. I told these intelligent young men and women that if they really wanted to do something great with their lives, they could start by going and helping these Lost Children who didn't know how to read and write. I told them, "You have everything, and these children have nothing. Give something of yourself and see how it affects your life."

At the end of my talk, the president of their society got up and said, "Mrs. Jones, we've decided that our organization is going to give 2,000 rand to Norman House in order to purchase books."

The membership chairman came up and said, "A group of us have decided we will go to the Norman House and teach them to read."

Then the lady who was in charge of the various Golden Key chapters said, "There are eleven other universities that have Golden Key chapters in South Africa. Will you please come back next year and give your message to them?"

I felt like saying, "It wasn't my message." It was Heavenly Father's message, but in trusting Him, I was able to be an instrument in His hands.

A Most Memorable Fireside

My most spiritual experience was at our last large youth fireside in Cape Town. I gave a talk entitled, "Satan's Great Lies." I had given this talk many times before. The talk ends with the idea that Satan's fourth and greatest lie is that there is no way out. I end the talk telling them there will always be a way out because Christ said, "I am the way" (John 14:6). There will always be a way—the way is the Atonement.

At the end of this presentation, I show a video portraying some of the miracles of Christ during His lifetime and of His atoning sacrifice and Resurrection. During the video, in the dark, I always close my eyes and pray for each of the youth at the fireside. I pray that they will be touched by the Savior's sacrifice and want to change their lives to live with Him as their focus.

This night something very special happened. During the video, as I began to pray for the youth of South Africa in the darkness with my eyes closed, I saw in my mind's eye, the Savior walking into the back of the chapel. I pictured Him walking from youth to youth placing His hands for a moment over one, and then moving to the next. I prayed, "Lord, I wish that this would really be happening."

Then I started to hear sniffing. It wasn't all over the chapel. The sniffing seemed to be moving in a line, row by row! Then I felt as if angels were filling the entire chapel. I guess some could say that I wanted to believe what my mind was creating, but I believe that a miracle was taking place. When the fireside was over, the youth came up and formed a line. Some were crying and others were silent. They just hugged me or each other and thanked me for coming. One boy said, "I feel that tonight my life has been changed."

My prayers had been answered, not just that night but during the entire trip. I didn't have to live even one day on my own strength. He was with me, guiding me to do His work in South Africa.

THE TRIAL

I arrived home in May. The trial for the lawsuit was scheduled to begin September 27th. By August, pre-trial preparations were on the agenda. This was a final settlement hearing. My attorneys had assured me many times that this hearing was only a formality. We were preparing for a full two-week trial.

As we went to the courthouse that day at 9 AM for the hearing, I could see that the demands of the other parties were far beyond what we were willing to pay. There were two sets of attorneys and a mediator that went in and out of the mediation room. By 4 PM, the mediator came out of the room and said, "It doesn't look like they're going to lower their demands in order to settle this lawsuit."

My attorneys responded, "Then let's go home!"

I excused myself and went into the restroom. In one of the stalls, I locked the door, folded my arms, and began to pray, remembering that special fireside in South Africa. "All these years, Heavenly Father, I have prayed for the youth during my talks and asked that the Savior might bless each one of them. I wanted them to know that He lives and loves them. I have never asked for this same blessing to help myself, but today I'm asking (by this time I was in tears) that the Savior's influence might be in that mediation room and touch the hearts of those involved that this lawsuit might end."

I went back into the courtroom to wait with my attorneys. Ten minutes later the mediator came out of the room with a shocked look on his face and said they had just decided to settle! My attorneys were patting themselves on the back and saying that the other parties that had filed the lawsuit had finally realized that they didn't have a case—our indisputable evidence made them back down.

I smiled, knowing in my own heart the truth. My prayer for help had been answered. "Be patient in afflictions, for thou shalt have many; but endure them, for, lo, I am with thee, even unto the end of thy days" (Doctrine and Covenants 24:8).

My gratitude was and is to this day overwhelming. I never thought it would end without a trial. There might have been an appeal and more years of stress and uncertainty. But it came to an end with the help of the Lord. My life now goes on, but my gratitude to the Lord will be unending.

I trust Him completely in all things, knowing that what He brings into my life will be for my good. Even in the most tragic times of our life and also in the very best times in our life, He will always be with us, always guiding us, loving us as we do all things with His Holy name.

"If I take the wings of the morning, and dwell in the uttermost parts of the sea; Even there shall thy hand lead me, and thy right hand shall hold me" (Psalm 139:9–10).

I met Ellen during Education Week. As she shared her story I couldn't hold back the tears. I hugged her, and she thanked me for listening and said, "Telling my story helps me to heal." Her story wasn't one that anyone could possibly forget. It has made an indelible mark in my memory.

Ellen was born in Chihuahua, Mexico, to an LDS family. She married Matt Jones in 1995. After just one year of marriage, their son, Alex, was born, and two years later, daughter Adri, joined their family. Ellen's story is heartbreaking, but her Job-like experience can teach us about trusting in the Lord. I share her story here with her permission.

ELLEN'S STORY

I met my husband, Matt, while we were both attending a singles ward in Las Vegas. We were married and went to live in Provo where we managed a motel. It was there that our son, Alex, and daughter, Adri, were born.

This was a busy time in our lives, but we enjoyed the children and had lots of family living nearby. On what would be our last weekend in Provo, Gramps came over to mow the lawn with his riding lawn mower.

Ellen and Matt Jones with Alex and Adri.

Gavin and Jared with Mom and Dad.

Three-year-old Alex wanted a ride, but the short ride wasn't enough. He was upset and crying. Matt comforted him, held him, and told him Gramps would be back for another ride soon.

On Sunday we went to church. That night—our last night—Adri was crying. I gave her a big hug, kissed her on the head, and held her in my arms.

The next day we got up early to get things ready to go to Lake Powell. I had sent Alex and Adri outside to play. Matt caught Alex putting sand in the lawn mower. He came in the house and said, "You might want to check on the children."

Moments later, I peeked out the window and asked how they were doing. I saw Alex, and he tried to tell me something, but I didn't understand what he was saying. I went about getting ready for our outing.

Five or ten minutes later, a guest came to our door and said, "There is smoke coming out of that building."

I ran outside and looked closely. The smoke was coming from the boiler room. It seemed like I was moving in slow motion. I began to pray for my children. "Oh, God, please no, please don't take my kids." In looking back, I must have known they were no longer here. They were in the hands of our Lord.

The boiler room was engulfed in flames. All of the housekeepers were asking, "Where are the kids?"

I called 911 and said, "There's a fire, and my kids are in there!" I'm sure I said more, but I do not remember.

There was a live power line involved. We just watched as fire fighters put out the flames. The fire chief told me he thinks my babies died quickly from smoke inhalation. My husband had wanted to go into the shed, but I kept pulling him back. It was too late, and I didn't want to lose him too.

When the yard was mowed the day before, I remember that I had left the gas can down on the floor. My husband usually mows the lawn and places the can of gas up on a high shelf. The children must have wandered into our storage shed, which also served as the boiler room. I think my Alex may have tipped over the gas can, which I had left on the floor, but I never allow myself to think of the "what if." I just can't go there in my mind.

Can you imagine the guilt that we both carry?

We didn't know what to do. Can you imagine how hard it was calling family members and telling them your two darling children are both gone? Everyone rallied around us and gave us love and whatever else they could think of. I have felt strength and prayers from people I don't even know.

We arranged to have blessings from the stake presidency. I don't remember those blessings. I just remember a vision I had while receiving one of those blessings. First a feeling of comfort, love, and joy overwhelmed me. I envisioned an older Alex and Adri running upstairs. Alex was holding her hand saying, "Come on, Adri, let's go. Let's get there first." Then they came to a calm, beautiful place where Jesus was waiting for them. They met, hugged, and Jesus asked how they were doing. Alex looked sad and said, "I'm okay." Adri said, "I miss my mommy and daddy, especially Daddy, because I love him so much!" The vision ended there.

This has been a heartbreaking chapter in my life. I engulfed myself in writing music and found comfort there. More than anything, it helps to share my story. It helps me heal.

I can't begin to express the gratitude in our hearts for all the loving hands that nurtured and loved our children. I hope we may never take the precious life that we are given for granted, that we may always remember that God sent His children to be taught and raised in His image. I hope that we may earn the right to have them as our eternal children in the life hereafter. We need to enjoy every moment now. Tomorrow does not matter unless we live, give, and love today.

Two years later, our family had another addition. Our sweet son, Jared, was born. He is a tender child and has brought us much joy. And two years after that, we had another son, Gavin. I love my children, all of them. What a blessing it is and continues to be to have been given two new spirits to raise. I have been excited and nervous to watch them grow. Once I realized that I needed to trust in the Lord, that these were God's children, things became easier. All I needed to do was go to the Lord and say, "Lord, this is your child. What should I do to help him?"

I love the gospel and anticipate the Second Coming, when Jesus, the one who has comforted me, loved me, and healed my soul, will come. I anxiously await the grand reunions that will take place.

Here is a portion of the song Matt and I wrote:

EMPTY ARMS

They were married and in their late twenties.
They'd been trying for more than five years.
But no baby had come, no daughter or son.
On their knees they prayed through their tears.
Chorus
Heaven help us, we don't understand.
How does this fit in your plan?
Lord, we give you these empty arms,
Please, fill them with love.
. . . They had started their own little family.
But now pictures are all that remain.
No laughter, no cries, no small tear, no good-byes.
And their heart cried the question in pain.
Chorus
Heaven help us, we don't understand.
How does this fit in your plan?
Lord, we give you these empty arms,
Please, fill them with love.

Chapter 11

THE GIFT OF PRAYER

A bishop recently told me he felt that the adversary was taking a new direction. Satan has always targeted our youth, but lately he seems to be focusing a lot of attention on the women. We're overwhelmed, bombarded with distractions, overtired, overworked, and simply frazzled by all that life demands—or seems to demand—of us. Satan loves this! Being too busy and/or too tired to pray suits perfectly the purposes of the adversary.

"For if ye would hearken unto the Spirit which teacheth a man to pray ye would know that ye *must* pray; for the evil spirit teacheth not a man to pray, but teacheth him that he must not pray" (2 Nephi 32:8; emphasis added). Indeed, prayer is our lifeline to God, and by closing down the lines of communication we will not be able to draw on the powers of heaven. How can we hear God's direction if we can't find time to be calm, quiet, pray, and then listen to the whisperings of the Spirit?

I still remember some of my most fervent prayers offered during my first marriage. When I was held at gunpoint on two different occasions, I said in the silent depths of my being each time, "Heavenly Father, are you there?" I did not hear an audible voice, but both times my spirit heard the whispers from heaven say, "Yes, Barbara, I am here." I felt that calm, warm feeling that comes from the Holy Ghost. Both times, the tears just streamed down my cheeks. It didn't matter to me at that moment if my husband pulled the trigger because I felt such peace and comfort knowing the Lord was there with me.

My Heavenly Father had heard my prayers and promised "I am with you alway, even unto the end of the world" (Matthew 28:20).

TWO-WAY PRAYER

I once heard a noted evangelist give a lecture series on two-way prayer. He started with a story about being on a high ladder, painting his house when the ladder collapsed and he crashed to the ground. He realized, as he was riding in the ambulance, that he could not move. He said, "Heavenly Father, are you there?" He heard Heavenly Father speak to his spirit, "Yes, Bob, I'm here."

"Heavenly Father, I can't move. Am I going to be okay?"

"Yes, Bob, you're going to be fine."

Listening to that lecture series, combined with my own experiences, inspired me to give the same challenge while speaking to a group of teenage girls. I said, "Go home and test what I have found to be true. Get down on your knees and ask, 'Heavenly Father, are you there?' Then wait; listen. You will hear in the silent depths of your mind, 'Yes, I'm here.'

"Of course, at first you'll just think, 'Oh, I only think I'm hearing His voice because Sister Jones told me I would.' Ask again. You will hear the same answer, 'Yes, I'm here.' At first only ask simple things that can elicit yes and no answers. 'Am I living my life the way you want me to live?' Then listen and wait. He will answer."

Heavenly Father does answer our prayers. Here is an excerpt of a letter I received from a teenage girl who did as I suggested:

"My dad had to be rushed to the hospital on Thursday where he stayed in intensive care for over a week. The cause is still unknown. The doctor only called it a raging virus. As I sat in the front seat of the ambulance next to my mom, I thought my dad was going to die. For the first time in my life, I faced a very critical situation. So, I did what you did when you were scared. I asked my Heavenly Father if He was there. He very plainly and clearly said to me, 'Yes, I'm here, and it's going to be all right.'

"My dad came home and is fine. I am closer to my Heavenly Father now more than ever. I learned to appreciate my parents. I now know for sure that Heavenly Father does hear and answer prayers."

My son-in-law, Shane, a family therapist, took the time to write me a beautiful letter concerning my grandson Taylor.

Taylor Adamson

"Recently one of our family home evening lessons was on prayer. We decided that we would feel closer to Heavenly Father and get more answers if we waited and listened at the end of family prayer. Despite the struggles, we have had some very good experiences with this practice.

"A few weeks later I was saying goodnight prayers with the children, and we agreed that we all would wait and listen to see if God would give us a message. Noël and I fell asleep on Taylor's bed. Taylor woke me up and said he got a message. I asked him what it was. Taylor said, 'I asked Heavenly Father if he could please find my Grandpa Hal in heaven and tell him I miss him. I asked Heavenly Father that if He found Grandpa Hal and told him my message would he tell me? Dad, I got a really warm tingly feeling, and I know Heavenly Father found Grandpa Hal.'"

GOD HEARS

God does hear and answer our prayers in many ways. "For the Lord God giveth light unto the understanding; *for he speaketh unto men according to their language, unto their understanding*" (2 Nephi 31:3; emphasis added).

Sometimes you will hear the still small voice, as I did when I was held at gunpoint. At other times, prayers may be answered through the scriptures. Still, others may be answered through a person, a priesthood blessing, or a song. Yes, God does speak to us according to our own understanding and in our own language.

Dede Day was born with the gift of singing. She started performing when she was in kindergarten and is an exceptional singer. She came to my home for training before a Miss America preliminary in her state. During her stay, we spoke often of God and Christ.

Singer/songwriter Kenneth Cope happened to be at my home at the same time, working on a special music project. Dede asked him to explain to her about a living prophet and the plan of salvation. As she was leaving, we gave her a CD to listen to on the airplane.

When she arrived home, she called and excitedly told me that she wanted to be baptized. "There was a song on that CD that you gave me in

which the lyrics said, 'He lives again for me, He said, Come follow me.'"
. . . She knew instantly what Christ was telling her. Soon, she was baptized. Yes, God had spoken to her according to her own understanding and in her own language.

THE PRAYERS OF OTHERS

How comforting it is when we are going through a difficult time to know that others are praying for us. It gives us courage to carry on.

My husband had been ill for thirteen years. During those years, countless people prayed for him. While I was at EFY one summer, Hal was in critical condition. My friend, Scott Anderson, was the director of the session. I told him about Hal's condition and that Hal wouldn't let me stay home with him. Hal would always say, "You can do more good there than you can here." Scott had 1,500 youth pray for my husband every day for the entire week.

When I returned home, the nurse met me at the door and said Hal had turned the corner for the better. What a comfort for us to realize that we don't need to be speaking at EFY and have 1,500 youth pray for us. We can call any temple and know that through the prayer roll, hundreds of people can be praying.

Another amazing answer to prayer during Hal's illness was when he had viral pneumonia and congestive heart failure. His condition was so grave that he was on oxygen full-time. Elder Robert E. Wells, Hal's closest friend, gave Hal a blessing. And in this blessing, as a General Authority of the Church, Elder Wells called down angels from the presence of Heavenly Father to minister to Hal. Hal lived for four more years after that blessing.

KEEP A PRAYER JOURNAL

As we renovated our office several years ago, I found a journal written twenty-four years before. On the cover was written, "Dear Heavenly Father Prayer Journal." I was not a member of the Church then, but I had asked Heavenly Father for help and would give Him updates on the progress of my requests. I was amazed that twenty to twenty-five years later, many prayers had been answered. I was astonished to read this entry (keep in mind that I was a Catholic at this time):

"Journal entry: 1980

"Dear Heavenly Father, my dream is to someday help women who are hurting, to help women find a place where they can come to feel better about themselves and to lose weight, where there are Christian classes with teaching on nutrition, etiquette, grooming, and exercise."

At that point in my life I had previously only trained beauty queens for Miss USA and Miss America pageants. My first program for women in general was initiated at the request of my stake president and was held in 1990 for the women in my stake. It was known as "Metamorphosis." Then in 1996 (sixteen years after I wrote that journal entry), I began directing a week-long annual retreat for women at BYU–Hawaii.

Before we were baptized, my husband and I were getting ready to build a home. It took a year to find a lot and even longer to get the plans drawn and approved. On August 6, 1980, I wrote in my prayer journal (please excuse the irreverent use of the word you; I was not yet a member):

"Thank you Lord for so many, many blessings. I received a letter that the city council would be turning down our house plan. I turn the house over to you, Lord, to be yours, and to be used for your glory. So, I call to you sincerely, and I know that you will hear my cries for help.

"August 8

"The house plans passed. Thank you for hearing my prayers about turning this house over to you, and thank you, Heavenly Father for giving me a special scripture today when I randomly opened my Bible. 'And the Lord said unto him, I have heard thy prayer and thy supplication, that thou hast made before me: I have hallowed this house, which thou hast built, to put my name there for ever; and mine eyes and mine heart shall be there perpetually' (1 Kings 9:3)."

We dedicated our home to Him before we moved in December of 1982, which was the same month we were baptized. There is a plaque on our door that says, "This house was built and dedicated to our Father in Heaven. We ask all those who enter it to pray that He will use it for His glory."

But, of course, Satan never gives up when anyone tries to do a good thing. You can't imagine all the adversities we faced. Our house is built on a hill, and a torrential rainstorm washed part of the hill away during construction. Two huge extra rooms had to be built under the main living area as support for the upper floor. We called them "future rooms." My husband was so upset because of the additional cost. He wanted to sell the house before we moved in. One day I went downstairs to one of our future rooms, knelt down, offered up a prayer, and I wrote in my journal:

"Thank you, Heavenly Father, for hearing my prayer today about these two extra rooms and for revealing to me that these two rooms are only part of your greater plan."

Today, more than twenty-five years later, one of these rooms houses the office for our private foundation, whose mission is "To enhance the quality of life for women of all ages throughout the world." The other room has been turned into an apartment for couple missionaries. Who would have ever believed that! I'm so grateful for my prayer journal.

If you will keep a prayer journal, you will be shocked and amazed at how often your prayers are answered.

Prayer and Adversity

Ann Dibb, daughter of President Thomas S. Monson, while moderating a panel called Strength and Wisdom through Experience said, "Sometimes as we live through a particularly difficult time, we might ask if it were possible to forgo the strength and wisdom that we might receive in the future and plead with our Heavenly Father to remove the burden from our lives in the present. But that is not the Lord's way. We must be reminded of the Lord's plan. We must humble ourselves and pray most fervently that the Lord will keep His promise and will lift us up and sustain us in our time of greatest need, for He is our Father and we are His daughters" (*Wives and Daughters of the First Presidency*. 1999. VHS.).

Adversity comes in many forms:

One dear friend, who went through years in an abusive marriage, said, "You know, in those years, I drew closer to my Heavenly Father. Just thinking about how I had to draw near to Him was worth what I went through."

A lady I met at Education Week came up after the class, after everyone had left the room, burst into tears, and said, "I don't know what to do. My husband is very much into pornography on the Internet. I just found out." She just sobbed. I responded, "Talk to your Father in Heaven. Pray to be close to Him and have the strength to know what to do."

Another sister approached me and said, "My husband was just called to be the stake president. He is a very prominent attorney in our town. He was only called for two months and had to be released because of an affair that had not been resolved." Then she started sobbing. I said, "Go to your Father in Heaven in prayer. Stay close to Him. He will be your Comforter."

A young woman at a conference, married for five years, handed me this letter. "I always have to be on the go. Work, work, work! I am up until eleven or twelve cramming in all I can before I go to bed. I hit the pillow at night and crash! Six AM comes, and I hit the ground running, saying a quick prayer. My husband and I have been trying to have children. Every Sunday in Relief Society, all the women talk about are their children. It feels like a knife right through the center of me. So, I run, run, run and don't stop because if I keep extra busy, I won't get depressed. Right? Ha! I have neglected me, and Satan is trying his hardest to jam those communication lines."

Yes, indeed, adversity is all around us; and sometimes, all we can do is pray and leave the rest up to the Lord.

WHEN ALL YOU CAN DO IS PRAY

I'd like to tell you about a woman I know, Claudia Goodman, and her husband, Steve, and their family of twelve children. They were blessed with great musical talent that they shared all over the world, promoting the importance of families. They even sang "I Am a Child of God" for the Pope!

One day, traveling home from a performance, Steve was in a car with five of their children, and Claudia followed behind with the other seven. A truck broadsided Steve's car, leaving it an unrecognizable, mangled mess. Three of the children died instantly, and Steve and the other two children were critically injured.

Claudia came on the wreckage a few minutes later and thought she recognized the car. As she realized it was her family, she said all she could do was pray, "Oh God, give me strength." She didn't know what else to do, so she began to pray with all her heart and mind. She said, "I was flooded with the warmest burning feeling I have ever experienced in my life. I felt comforted as I heard Heavenly Father say over and over, 'Your children are in my hands.'"

Claudia's husband, Steve, said, "Sooner or later this type of experience will come to all of us. It is one of the greatest lessons of life to know that Heavenly Father will always be there, that our families are the essence of our happiness and the fortress of our love. There was a time when I didn't think I could be as grateful for this difficulty and tragedy as I am today. But I think our life has been blessed because of this adversity, and it has given us a greater bond of love and respect and commitment to stay closer as a family than we have ever had."

Prayer is our lifeline to God, a personal connection to the powers of heaven. One of the greatest improvements we can make in our lives is to strengthen our prayer life. We learn that our greatest comfort comes in drawing close to Heavenly Father in prayer and taking the time to truly listen when He answers.

On an April night in a chapel in Durban, South Africa, halfway around the world from Church headquarters, a slim woman made her way up to the podium after my fireside. She introduced herself and told me briefly of her own past as a ballerina and her frightening experiences that paralleled some of my own: being held at gunpoint, reaching out desperately to Heavenly Father in prayer, and finally facing the tragedy of death.

I later heard her full story and knew it was the story that truly exemplified the power of prayer. I share it here with her permission.

SHANNON VAN ZYL'S STORY

I was born in Zimbabwe, the only child of two wonderful people.

Shannon Van Zyl

When I was nineteen, my parents and I joined the Church. Shortly thereafter, I met the love of my life, Gavin. He was a jockey and was also a member of the Church. We became husband and wife a year after we met. I gave up my ballet career and dedicated my life to being a wife and mother.

Three years later we were blessed with a beautiful baby girl whom we named Melissa. We both wanted a large family, so we were delighted when less than two years later Gareth was born. We were on a roll. Within ten years, we had six beautiful children: Melissa, Gareth, Chesney, Derek, Richard, and Felicity.

This story starts when Derek was a baby, and I intended to make a quick trip to the shopping center. I usually left the children with our housekeeper, but because my other three children were not at home, I decided to take Derek with me.

After finishing my purchases, I made my way quickly back to our Volkswagen microbus. It was nearly five o'clock, and I would hit the rush hour traffic. Derek was a routine-oriented baby and would soon need his bath and feeding. I also had dinner to prepare.

I opened the sliding door of the vehicle and buckled Derek into his baby seat. As I made my way around to the driver's side, I was approached by a man pointing a gun at me. I couldn't believe that this was happening to me. It was something you read about in the news or see in the movies, but you never think it will happen to you.

"Is this a real gun?" I looked into the barrel and saw that it did indeed have bullets.

The man ordered me into the microbus, but I refused. So many things went through my mind, but I remember thinking that I didn't want to get in because I was so afraid of what this person would do to me. Yet, I didn't want to leave Derek there alone. At this moment I looked up to the heavens and said, "Heavenly Father, please help me." At the time I had no idea just how powerful that simple, short prayer was.

I ran toward the back of the vehicle screaming for someone to help me when I heard the gunshot. I felt something hit me in the back, and I knew it must have been a bullet. I leaned against the car, expecting to fall. I felt for blood, but there was nothing.

By this time the man got into my microbus and was pointing the gun toward Derek. I screamed even louder. Suddenly, I felt a bullet hit my lower jaw, and I fell to the ground. Within seconds the hijacker was off in my vehicle with my thirteen-month-old baby still strapped in his car seat in the back.

I don't know how many people were near me trying to help. My jaw was loose, and I struggled to speak. Somehow I was able to tell them that Derek had been taken. I wrote down my phone number, and my husband, Gavin, was contacted. Mental images of my husband, my children, and my family filled my mind. It's amazing how by just thinking of the ones you love, you are able to gather so much strength and perseverance. At the hospital, my stake president gave me a special blessing telling me to be calm, that Derek was safe, and I would be spared.

Gavin went from radio station to television station to broadcast the story and plead with the public to help us find our baby boy. I was taken into surgery. When I was still in a semi-comatose state, Gavin came and told me that they had found Derek. Oh the joy. Our baby was back. I wanted to see him, to touch him, to know for myself that he was fine. Millions prayed that we could find Derek. They all knew that only Heavenly Father could make this miracle happen.

I was told what had happened. Three men had found Derek at ten o'clock at night wandering in the middle of the road five hours after he had been taken. They recognized him as the child they had seen on television and took him to the police. One of the rescuers said he came within inches of knocking him down. He swerved just in time. It was presumed that he had been left at the side of the road because a white hat and a blanket had also been found. One amazing thing was that a few paces away from where he had been left, there was an open manhole cover. Had Derek fallen into it, we may never have found him. Again, more answers to prayer!

I underwent eight operations. A section of my lower jaw had been shot away, so I had to have a bone graft from my hip. My mouth was wired shut for nine weeks. Later, teeth were implanted into the new jaw, and I was at last able to talk, to taste, to swallow, and to chew. To this day, I am so appreciative that I survived with so few bad side effects.

I returned home and found that I was often light-headed and dizzy. I went to the doctor and was told I was pregnant! It seems I was two weeks pregnant at the time of the hijacking. I was so worried about all the drugs and medications that I had been given and the X-rays that were done during my stay in the hospital. What effect would all this now have on this new baby? I still had more operations to undergo. The timing could not have been worse. But I would later discover the timing was perfect. I had a Heavenly Father who knew everything.

My second son, Chesney, had to be operated on for a pulmonary artery that was narrowing. The time he needed the operation was now, just a month after the news of a new baby. Chesney went into surgery and had a remarkable recovery.

Things seemed to be going well, I was recovering, and the family was together. One day I had left the three little boys at home playing with their dad, and I took Melissa to ballet. When I arrived home, I knew something was wrong because Gavin was waiting for me at the outside gate looking shocked and concerned. Someone had been injured. Surely it could not be Derek. But yes, it was Derek. A terrible accident had occurred where the automatic garage door had been activated and came down on Derek's head. He had been airlifted to the hospital. Gavin was once again put through terrible emotion and panic. It was peak traffic hour, and we had to be patient getting to the hospital. I kept asking Gavin if he thought Derek was alive. He said he didn't know, but deep down he knew. I never again want to go through the experience of walking into a hospital with hope and fear and then be taken privately into a room and be told that my child was dead.

Derek died and was buried two days later. I had days where I was angry and confused. I missed my child, and I felt I had been robbed because I had to have other people care for him while I recovered from my injuries. I wanted him back. I wanted to tell him how much I loved him. I spent time wondering why, after all the previous trauma, would Derek be taken now? I know that it would have been a terrible trial for us if we had never found Derek, not knowing if he was dead or alive or how he had been treated. I know that Heavenly Father responded to the prayers of all those wonderful people. All I know is that Derek was indeed a special child and was sent to teach us lessons that we could never have learned without him. It was a privilege to be chosen to be the parents of this little boy. His beautiful big, blue eyes, his warm blonde hair, and his wide open smile will forever live in my memory.

The new baby, Richard Derek James, was born ten weeks early at 2.2 pounds. But he was perfect. I was not given time to hold him after his birth because he had to be whisked off to the premature unit. His middle name was for his brother, but we refer to him as Richard the Lionhearted.

I then realized how wise our Heavenly Father really was. I had thought that the timing of this pregnancy was terribly wrong, but, in fact, the time was perfect. Heavenly Father, in His great wisdom and love, knew how hard it would be to accept the death of Derek, so we were given another, not to replace him, but another to love who could help heal a broken heart.

Richard progressed well, and he was almost a year old when we discovered that yet another baby was to join our family. This little spirit decided that she, too, wanted an early start. As hard as the doctors tried, they could not hold this baby back. On Derek's birthday, Felicity was born. You can call it coincidence, but I call it a miracle.

I am grateful for my loving Heavenly Father who has always answered my humble prayers, and for the wonderful family that He has blessed me with—a family who loves me for who I am and who support me through good times and bad—and for the opportunity that we have in life to try to become more like the Savior. I'm grateful for the thousands of people who have prayed for us and those who have helped us on our way.

Chapter 12

THE GIFT OF LOVE

As we read the scriptures, we often don't really understand the true nature of our Savior and just how much He loves us. When Jairus' daughter had died and the Savior was told of her death, He said, "Be not afraid, only believe" (Mark 5:36).

Then the Savior went to the little girl. There she was, twelve years old, lying in the bed, and she was dead. What did He do?

"And he took the damsel by the hand, and said unto her, Talitha cumi; which is, being interpreted, Damsel, I say unto thee, arise" (Mark 5:41).

When we read that verse, it sounds very commanding, like the narrator in a big movie: "DAMSEL, I say unto thee ARISE."

But, looking at the true etymology of the words *Talitha cumi* sheds a lot of light on the Savior's kindness. In Aramaic, the words are more accurately translated as, "Get up, little lamb" (see *Zondervan Pictorial Bible Dictionary,* 827). Ahhh. Now we have a glimpse of the nature of our Savior as kind, compassionate, and loving.

In John 8:3–11, when the woman who was taken in adultery was brought to Jesus, He could have chastised her for breaking the law of Moses or chastised the crowd for troubling him, but instead he said to the angry crowd, "He that is without sin among you, let him first cast a stone at her" (John 8:7). He looked down and wrote on the ground, and when he looked up the crowd was gone. He said to her, "Woman, where are those thine accusers? hath no man condemned thee?" She answered, "No man, Lord" to which he softly and lovingly replied, "Neither do I condemn thee: go, and sin no more" (John 8:10–11). Once again, we feel Christ's love and compassion.

Elder David B. Haight shared this story about President Spencer W. Kimball: "I often think of the time President Spencer W. Kimball . . . called me to the temple. I was busy as an Assistant to the Twelve at that time, and he telephoned me to meet him at the fourth floor of the temple. He said, 'David, can you come right now?' And I said, 'Yes, President.' And he said, 'Right now.' And as I walked to the temple, my heart was beating fast, not knowing, of course, what President Kimball was calling me there for.

"But he took me into a room that I hadn't been in before, and there President Kimball interviewed me regarding my worthiness. And, of course, I was amazed because of his speaking to me that way, because I didn't have any idea why I was there. And then he motioned for us to stand, and as I was standing with that wonderful man and he's holding my hands, he said to me, 'With all the love that I possess, I'm calling you to fill the vacancy in the Quorum of the Twelve Apostles.' And when he said that, I thought I would collapse with the shock, the astonishment that came into my mind!

"And so, as I had sleepless nights after that call, I mulled that in my mind and I have thought of it time and time again. He did not say, 'As the

President of the Church' or 'As the prophet' or 'By my authority.' He said, in that humble, humble way of his, 'With all the love that I possess.' He was teaching me that love is essential—the love that the Savior hopes that we will acquire—that we must show, that we must demonstrate, we must feel in our hearts and souls . . ." ("Special Witnesses of Christ," *Ensign,* April 2001, 12–13).

Hal and I had our own special experience with President Kimball, and cherish the opportunity we had to feel the love of Christ radiating from a prophet of God. Right after my husband and I were baptized, we received a phone call from Elder Clausen, the missionary who baptized us. He said, "Brother and Sister Jones, I'm going to get married, and I would like it if you would come to Salt Lake and meet my fiancée."

We asked him to pick a restaurant where we could meet. He chose the restaurant overlooking the temple. It was late afternoon, and as the elevator doors opened, the area before the restaurant was nearly empty. We saw an elderly gentleman hunched over his cane, sitting on a bench.

Elder Clausen said, "That's President Kimball."

Elder Clausen walked over and introduced himself and his fiancée first, and President Kimball smiled. Then Elder Clausen said, "I would like for you to meet Sister Jones. We baptized the Jones family on my mission." I shook his hand, and he smiled.

Hal was next. Now, Hal was a businessman. He walked over to President Kimball with his determined manly stride and extended his hand. It was as if time stood still, just as when Jesus was looking into the eyes of the woman of Samaria and could see all the things she had ever done. So it seemed that President Kimball looked into my husband's eyes.

Finally, after what seemed like an eternity, he reached up, put his arms around Hal's neck, and drew him down to his knees in front of him. He embraced Hal, kissed him, and said three times softly, "I love you."

My husband slowly stood and walked to our table. He was as white as a sheet, and so was I. As we sat down, Hal said, "I have just met a prophet of God."

I will never forget the feeling we both had that memorable day. It was undeniable. Our testimony of a prophet of God was made, and it was based on love, the pure love of Christ, which radiated from President Kimball as the Savior's representative.

God's Love for You

What tells you there is a God? Just look at a single flower and notice the delicate markings, the absolute perfection of the colors and design. When my granddaughter, Eliza, was a little girl and I was taking her for a walk in her stroller, I stopped to pick a beautiful pink zinnia and handed it to her. She smiled and sniffed deeply with her nose on the center of the flower. She said, with her precious lisp, "Gram-B, it is t-so beau-t-ful."

I said, "Did you know that Heavenly Father made this flower, and I picked it today as a present to you from Him?"

She looked seriously into my eyes, with her hand now strangling the zinnia and said, "Gram-B, I going to keep this frow-wa fo-ev-a."

Yes, there is a God, and I am completely overwhelmed by the love that He has for each of us individually. Sometimes it is difficult to understand how Heavenly Father would have enough time to hear and know of our needs at any given moment. How can He possibly help just me when there are so many billions of people on this earth?

I love the following passages of scripture, which answer this question.

"Then shall ye call upon me, and ye shall go and pray unto me, and I will hearken unto you. And ye shall seek me, and find me, when ye shall search for me with all your heart. And I will be found of you" (Jeremiah 29:12–14).

In Matthew 7:7 we read, "Ask, and it shall be given unto you; seek, and ye shall find; knock, and it shall be opened unto you."

All you have to do is ask. How magnificent is that! All we have to do is do such a simple thing. And then His love will be poured out on us.

And that is also the beauty of our gratitude to Him. When He hears and answers our prayers, we are most grateful and want to help Him in return. Help Him, by being His hands, His voice, and His feet here upon this earth.

I think back on two recent memorable examples of God hearing the desires of my heart and answering me, and then in turn allowing me to be an instrument in His hands for someone else.

I had been speaking for the Church for over twenty years, but when the invitation from Church Public Affairs in South Africa came, I had trepidation—South Africa! One of my first venues in Johannesburg was the opportunity to speak with President Steven Snow, the Area President, to discuss the tour with him. I was excited. My prayer from the tour's inception, which occurred a year earlier, was that I would be able to share my testimony and love of the gospel with this special man. I wanted him to know my story of abuse: the suicide death of my first husband, my subsequent marriage to a wonderful man with whom I raised my children, and how as a family we found the gospel of Jesus Christ. Now I spend my life serving my Heavenly Father with the help of our foundation. It is the mission of our foundation to help women of all ages to reach their potential.

The day before I left I received my final itinerary. My time with the

Area President had been cut to ten or fifteen minutes due to a change in his schedule. I was just heartsick. Hadn't God heard my prayer? Didn't He know how important this was to me? To make a very long story short, I never quit praying about this meeting.

When the day came, my liaison with Public Affairs said that my time had been cut to just about five minutes. It was unavoidable, but the President just didn't have any time for private meetings that day. I understood. I had been asked the night before to speak to a small group of Church employees about the possibility of doing a youth conference in South Africa. When I arrived at the Church area office, which was on the same grounds as the Johannesburg South Africa Temple and the "white house"—the name given to the Area President's home—I was ushered down a hallway to a door. When the door was opened, I was in shock! There sitting in neat rows were all of the Church employees and missionaries, and in the front row was President Snow and his lovely wife. The president welcomed me, and I nervously disclosed to him that no one had told me that I would be giving a talk here today. With a smile, President Snow said, "Sister Jones, I'm sure that Heavenly Father will direct you."

Then it hit me! "Oh, Heavenly Father, You did it again! You did hear my prayer! You did realize how important this was to me, and now you are making it possible for me to tell my story, my conversion, and my testimony." When I came to an ending point, I looked at the President, and he said, "Go ahead and take about fifteen more minutes." Of course, I was not at a loss for words.

That night as I sat in the darkness in my hotel room, I cried. "How wonderful you are, Father, to have found such an ingenious way to answer my prayer. If I had known ahead of time I would have worried for days." I'm sure that what happened that day wasn't important in the overall scheme of the entire tour, but He knew it was important to me. That trip taught me to rely on my Father in Heaven each and every day of the entire five weeks. I had absolutely no time to prepare before each talk, but I have never felt the Spirit so strongly.

The stunning experience of being close to our Heavenly Father is to receive His love, whether from Himself or others, and to be lifted ourselves by it. Then we can try to be to them as He has been to us, lifting and blessing them with our love in turn. The gift of love comes from the Savior himself: "A new commandment I give unto you, That ye love one another as I have loved you, that ye also love one another" (John 13:34). Pass it on.

In April of this year I received an e-mail from my friends, Deb and Wayne, who were serving as a senior missionary couple in the Seoul Korea Mission. "Hi Barbara, we need for you to come to Seoul, Korea, on May 25–27 for our big singles conference. We have prayed and prayed for guidance in this matter, and your name keeps coming up."

I thought as I read, "Deb, you know me. My schedule is booked a year in advance." I looked at my calendar and on that date I had a very important wedding to attend of a girl who is like a daughter to me. I could never cancel and not be there on her wedding day.

I told my daughter, Wendy, about my invitation to Seoul. The next day the bride-to-be, Sarah, called. "Barbara, you have to go to Korea. God wants you to go; I just know He does." (Now, I've seldom heard Sarah bring up the subject of God, even though she came from a very Christian background.) "And I want you to go. You will be at my wedding in spirit."

I hung up the phone and quickly sent another e-mail. I felt, without a doubt, that Heavenly Father was opening a door for me to go.

When I arrived in Seoul it was evening. Deb and Wayne were there with smiles on their faces to pick me up. What a grand reunion we had !

The next morning we were going to do a session at the Seoul Korea Temple. I was so excited to be there. I wanted to pinch myself. Just as we were leaving for the temple, the mission president called to tell Deb and Wayne that one of their new sister Missionaries (she had only been in Seoul for five weeks) had just asked to go home. The mission president said that she would be in our same temple session and that maybe they could talk with her.

As we traveled to the temple, they told me that this girl was so darling. She was from Arizona, had flaming red hair, and her name was Sister McDowell.

We arrived, changed our clothing, and went to wait in the chapel. I looked around to see how many people would be in the session. As I looked to my right, I saw all of the elders sitting in their pews. I felt tears welling up in my eyes. They looked so young, so handsome, so filled with the Spirit, and here they were so far away from home, giving two years of their lives to serve their Heavenly Father.

The session seemed more beautiful to me than ever. As I sat at the end of the session in the celestial room, I thanked my Heavenly Father for opening the doors for me to come these thousands of miles to a place that I never dreamed of coming. I asked Him for guidance to help me with the singles conference. (Some of the singles would be driving five hours to this conference.) I felt some inspiration about the conference, but nothing profound.

Then as I looked across the room, I saw the sister with the flaming red hair—Sister McDowell. I said a quick prayer and asked Heavenly Father if there was anything that I might say to her. More clearly than I could ever describe, I heard these words, "*She* is the reason that I brought you here"!

All of this way for *one* young girl, because her Father in Heaven loved her so dearly. I stood up, walked over to her, and knelt down by her side. Her head was down, and she was crying. I could only imagine the confusion and turmoil that she must have been feeling. I introduced myself to her and asked if she and her companion could come and have lunch with us at the senior missionary couple's apartment. She whispered to her companion, and they accepted the invitation.

As we arrived at the apartment, I could see that the lunch preparations would take a while. I asked Sister McDowell if she would come to my room and talk to me. All I remember saying to her was, "Why don't you tell me your story." She started by telling me that she knew that she was supposed to come to Korea on her mission. When she received her call, she knew that this was where Heavenly Father wanted her to go. She said that everything had fallen into place for her once she had made the decision to go. She had sold her car right away, and she was able to lease her apartment without a problem. When her call came everyone told her that they felt so good about her being called to Seoul. She said that during her mission farewell, she felt complete peace. Her parents were happy for her. Her brother told her that he had never been happier than while serving a mission.

In the Missionary Training Center she had felt good about learning the language, but when she got to Seoul everything changed. She said, "I can't speak the language; it's just too hard. I'm not happy like my brother said that he was, but the biggest thing is . . . I feel that God doesn't even know who I am!"

The tears started to stream down my cheeks as I told her about my experience in the temple. Then I said, "My dear Sister McDowell, your Father in Heaven loves you so dearly that He sent me all this way, thousands of miles, just to let *you* know how much He cares about you. You are His daughter! I pray that for the rest of life you will never forget this." We hugged and cried together, and she told me she would stay.

This experience truly exemplifies the royal law, "As I have loved you . . . love one another" (John 13:34). As our Heavenly Father and our Savior, Jesus Christ, have loved me, so must I love others. When I do, the love will never end. We must become part of this eternal plan. We must be like earthly angels. As part of your divine destiny, He will put people in your life to help guide you in the right direction, and you in turn will influence the life of someone else for good. "By this shall all men know that ye are my disciples, if ye have love one to another" (John 13:35).

I met Susan at Education Week. I had just come from a meeting, and as I walked out of the building, I came face to face with a woman using a cane. For some reason, I stopped and asked her about her condition. (I had needed a cane when I was in severe pain and in need of a hip replacement.) When she told me her story, of living through a tragic accident, becoming a paraplegic, and the suicide death of her son, I told her that I felt that our meeting had not been accidental. Maybe hers was the story that needed to end this book. Yes, it was a story of love, the love of a Heavenly Father for His daughter throughout the course of her life. A love that helped her survive the refiner's fire. I share it here with her permission.

SUSAN KESSLER'S STORY

Susan Kessler today

I was born in a little hospital in Arcadia, California, the middle of five children. My mother called me her wild horse because I was born across the street from a racetrack. We were very different from each other, and a wise Heavenly Father must have put us together to teach us.

My father achieved a high degree of success in the business world. This success afforded us a lifestyle that most can only dream of, but we also had a father who worked long hours and a mother who was depressed. From anyone else's perspective, I was a girl who had everything. Yet, like my mother, I too was depressed. My mother's constant nagging as well as her angry looks made me want to be anywhere but home. I would ask over and over if I could live in a foster home. I'm sure I didn't know what I was asking; however, I know what I wanted—love.

Finally, my parents found a home for me with another LDS family. In fact, the father was the bishop of our ward. But it was the mother, Sister Poole, to whom I became very attached. We would talk about everything, and we seemed to be kindred spirits.

One night when their daughter, Lori, was out (we shared a room), I sat on the bed looking out the window. It was dark and raining outside. I was lonely and felt sad. I also had an ear infection. It had ached on and off, but it wasn't until I was sitting there looking out the window that the pain became unbearable. As I closed my eyes and held my throbbing ear, I prayed in desperation. I asked God to help me with this mounting pain.

Then, as soon as I voiced this plea, the pain in my ear vanished. Even more remarkable, it didn't return. But this wasn't the miracle. As I sat there marveling at what had just happened, my eyes still closed, I began to experience an overwhelming sensation of love that seemed to envelop me. Somehow I felt as if I were being held in the arms of my Heavenly Father. At the same time I also felt His sadness for me. In fact, I could sense that He was crying. I can't explain how I experienced these things. I just did. And feeling His tears and love for me I, too, began to cry from the depths of my being. Then I knew that my Father in Heaven loved me, and I also knew beyond any doubt that I was His daughter.

As I opened my eyes, the entire room appeared misty. My aching heart was now filled with peace, and I walked out of my room to find Sister Poole. She was in the basement folding laundry, and when she saw me, she knew that something had happened. I cried as I shared with her my sweet experience, and she cried too.

As I worked with Bishop Poole, I was soon prepared to receive my patriarchal blessing, which has since become my most prized possession. Even though there were things written in my blessing that would take a lifetime to understand, there were also sweet and tender words confirming to me that I indeed had a Father in Heaven who loved me very much and that He had an important mission for me to fulfill.

I moved back to my home after living with the Pooles and dived into activity in the Church. All my recreational activities now seemed to be centered on the Church and the people in it.

It was during this time that I met Darrell, a handsome, clever, and persistent young man. He was twenty-two and had not gone on a mission.

In fact, he was just starting to come back to church. He would often smell of cigarettes, but who was I to judge? Besides, he made my heart pound. We dated for ten months and then became engaged to be married in the Los Angeles California Temple.

One Saturday afternoon, my sister asked to have a very important talk with me. She confided that with sincere prayer offered in my behalf, I should not marry Darrell. She had felt frustrated and angry about the way he treated me. Her words somehow penetrated my soul and rang true. That night I gave Darrell back his ring. A short time later, he made the decision to go on a mission. I promised to write.

No sooner had he left then I met Terry. He was tall and cute, with that all-American look, and had recently returned from a mission. "What a catch!" We quickly became an "item." As we continued to date, his goodnight kisses gave me the distinct impression that we were moving out of the friendship phase and toward something more.

One beautiful autumn day we decided to drive up in the mountains to see the changing leaves. Ascending the winding road up the mountainside, we laughed and flirted. I could never have imagined that I would not be coming back down the same way we went up. Several hours later a helicopter would take me down this same mountain. I had fallen from the rock Terry and I decided to climb. While lying in the midst of rocks and brush, my mind considered the possibilities of my condition, and my thoughts turned to my Heavenly Father. Even as I prayed desperately for the strength and courage to withstand the test I sensed was before me, a very distinct feeling filled my entire soul. I became aware that a question or choice was being placed before me as an inaudible yet very real voice communicated to me, "Susan, do you want to live?"

As I contemplated this question, my mind became opened in the most miraculous way. It was like I was standing in the middle of a flat desert and seeing ahead and behind me a never-ending stretch of land with nothing to obstruct my view. It was a profound glimpse of eternity, and it was vast.

Then, in the center of this vastness was a very small speck of time. This little speck of time was this earth life. I saw this life between birth and death to be miniscule. The unique wonder and importance of this life was that every moment, every day, every breath was a precious gift that was to be cherished. Nothing worldly could compare to life itself. And even though this life was a small speck compared to the vastness of eternity, it was not to be wasted. A great desire and respect for this life grew within me.

During this period I was always aware of my body and the choice that had been given to me. I thought about my accident, and I knew that it was serious—serious enough to choose to die. I didn't know details about my condition, but my mind began to speculate. I considered the worst. Yet, as I considered my physical condition in the context of this magnificent eternal view, it held absolutely no weight in making this decision. My physical condition seemed to be completely insignificant compared to the joy and privilege of this life. All of the physical limitations we have here are so very temporary, and I realized that everyone has them in this life. It didn't matter if mine were more or less than anyone else's. In fact, our physical infirmities or other trials were as much a part of the wonder of this life as anything more blatantly beautiful or good.

Every fiber of my being wanted to be a part of this life and my soul screamed from the deepest part of me, "Yes, Heavenly Father, I want to live!"

At that moment, I knew as well as I had ever known anything before that I would have my desire—that I would live. After my initial examination, the doctor told my parents that I would probably not make it through the night. Later my parents were told that I would live, but I would never walk again, as I was paralyzed from my waist down. But I knew differently.

I would live the next three months in hospitals. Along with my broken back and broken rib, I would also face a broken heart as Terry and I would go our separate ways.

A year after my accident I was walking with a limp, which I have to this day. When Darrell came home from his mission, I married him a month later in the Los Angeles California Temple. I spent the next two years and two pregnancies going back and forth with a man who had an uncontrollable temper and was addicted to pornography. He beat me and belittled me repeatedly. I finally divorced him by the time my second son was born. I spent the next year and a half fighting Darrell in court trying to protect my sons. When this didn't work, I tried to find a man to marry and protect us from him.

After two failed relationships, I began to put my life back together. I went back to school, joined a health club, brought my boys to church, and prayed. I eventually met and married my husband of twenty-one years. His name is Randy. His heart was broken, and his children were back east with his ex-wife and the man for whom she left him. But Randy was a good man, and we both knew we were meant to put all these broken hearts together, and we were married.

Since then we have gone through years of trials. My oldest son, Darrick, and two of Randy's daughters were all heroin addicts at one point. All three lived with us during their drug use. Yet we have been blessed to bring two more children into this world. When Randy and I were sealed in the Los Angeles California Temple, I knew that this very special man would always walk on the right hand of the Savior. My life had been blessed with his tenderness, love, and caring.

During the following summer I went through chemotherapy and radiation treatments because of a cancerous tumor found in my colon. When I had no strength left in my crippled body after coming home from my cancer treatments, I knew that I at least had the strength to pray and read my scriptures daily. I grew to love this time I spent with my Father. It became the very water to which I needed to live through a day, the water to live with His spirit

Little did I know that all of my previous tests were only to prepare me for a phone call I would get a year later. A call from a distraught daughter-in-law told me that Darrick, my twenty-five-year-old son, had died from a heroin overdose. "It's okay, it's okay," I kept saying, as Haddie screamed in hysteria.

How could I handle such a thing? How could I say that it was okay? It was He who held me up once again. It was He, the Father of my spirit, who cradled me in his arms and cried for me. But now I had learned to do my part. I had learned to put oil in my lamp for such a day as this.

On the backside of Darrick's funeral program I included a poem I had written, a poem about grief.

Grief

I sit and stare, I cry, I pray, and then I move for just a
while, and then I stop and stare and pray. My pain feels heavy.
Life seems to have halted somehow and then it starts again,
and I can move. Oh grief, old friend, it has been a while. I have
managed to avoid your sober face, now I must look into your

eyes once more. You have taught me much in years past, now I must be schooled again, old teacher.

Don't let me drown in the depths of your gripping waters. Teach me what I have come here for and then let go so I can swim free. Oh please, old friend, let go. I think of other's heartaches and mine is not as much. I think of His pain in that ancient garden so long ago and I have not bled from even one small pore. Yet you bring me to His holy feet and somehow and in someway our union, old teacher, becomes sweet.

Please make my spirit contrite and take this broken heart as my gifts to Him. And when I am finally free from your tight hold and you hide your face once more from my view, I pray I may walk a little closer to Him. I then will be grateful for this time we spent. For I have come to know, old friend, that what now feels like a deep slice in the center of my heart, that you are really the knife in the master jeweler's hand. And when my wound heals, as I know it will, instead of a bitter scar, I pray it may heal clear and straight and give me a little more depth and luster. In that day, old friend, when you let go.

I can testify that this old friend has indeed let go, and in its place I feel God's love and joy—the joy that I was shown thirty years ago as the sun was setting behind an autum-colored mountain. Years that "passed away . . . as it were unto [me] a dream" (Jacob 7:26; emphasis added). Thank you, Father, for giving me the eyes to see this joy and to feel your love.

Epilogue

ESPECIALLY FOR YOU

Thirty years ago, my dear friend, a young Catholic nun, told me the story of her first ten-day retreat of complete silence. As I wrote this book, I felt impressed that this story would be the perfect ending for this book—a gift especially for you, the reader.

I had filed the story away in my mind, but as I began to write about it, I wondered about the details that were missing. I tried to put myself in her place and live her story. How did she feel when she walked into the countryside? I went to the countryside to see for myself. As I began to feel and write the details of this unique adventure with nature, I have never felt God's presence more strongly. The tears would stream down my cheeks as I drenched myself in the beauty of His creation. I stayed for many days and nights, and my final night it rained, and when I left to go back home there appeared the magnificent rainbow of which the story speaks.

I now truly believe that this young nun's experience was meant for all of us. It is my prayer that it will touch your life as it has touched mine.

THE SILENT RETREAT

My friend, Sister Donna Marie, was with the Catholic order of nuns known as the Sisters of Mercy, the same order that I had lived with in New York.

In Northern California, in the countryside, rests a beautiful home reserved especially for retreats. Donna had been worried because her first silent retreat of ten days was about to begin. She was young, filled with energy and enthusiasm, and talked non-stop. She didn't think she could possibly last for ten days of just sitting in a wooden, straight-backed cubicle without saying a word.

The first day could only be described as frustrating. She fidgeted with her hands and couldn't sit still. Her mind raced with a million things she needed to do and problems that were happening with members of her family. It seemed that the silent ten days would be excruciatingly difficult.

The second day she begged Heavenly Father in prayer to please teach her some wonderful lesson during these nine remaining days. The following day, as she prayed, she saw in her mind's eye a large, black wrought-iron birdcage and in it was a wild, black bird. She watched the wild bird as it bashed its wings against the bars of the cage with such force that the bird would surely destroy itself. As she watched the scene, she realized that the wild bird was merely a representation of herself.

The fourth day, as she prayed and watched the wild bird, she heard the still small voice telling her, "Be still, and know that I am God" (Psalm 46:10). Immediately the bird stopped its destructive behavior and rested peacefully on the swing in the cage. Not a feather moved! Donna suddenly felt complete peace wash over her entire being. She sat in the wooden cubicle for the remainder of the day and basked in the stillness, calm, and serenity.

The fifth and sixth days, enveloped with this peace, she walked into the countryside beyond the gates of the house. She knelt down in the wet grass next to the poppies and was "still." She noticed for the first time the detail of the brilliant red saucer-like pedestals upon which the orange blossom of the poppy rested. Overhead in perfect formation, with the precision of an arrow, flew a gaggle of geese. A meadowlark swirled, lilted, swooped, and sailed off into the blue. The sky behind the bird was watermelon pink, streaked with gold. The air seemed sweet with the fragrance of minted grass and blooming narcissus. She watched the stream as the clear, glistening water danced atop mossy rocks and the smoky, white clouds like puffy pieces of cotton candy drifted softly atop dark green hills. "Be still, and know that I am God" . . . and she knew.

On the seventh day, once again in the wooden cubicle, she saw in her mind's eye a beautiful waterfall cascading from high atop a pine-clad mountain with the water crashing down on the rocks below. It was revealed to her that the waterfall represented the outpouring of God's love.

The eighth day she saw once again the magnificent falls; but now she was drawn to the bottom of the falls where the water churned with a white, effervescent foaming spray, and she knew that the bubbling white foam was the joy that is felt from the outpouring of God's love to us.

With the ninth day, came a final part of this scene. She saw the waterfall (God's love), the foam at the bottom (the joy we feel when receiving the outpouring of God's love), and then a stream that ran from the base of the falls further than the eye could see. It was revealed to her that the stream represented giving—giving of oneself to others. And she knew that her prayer had been answered, and a profound life lesson had been learned: "Be still, and know that I am God." See with spiritual eyes all the magnificent beauty of nature that surrounds you.

With her heart and spirit filled to overflowing, she awakened the final morning to the comforting sound of rain softly falling on the wooden porch outside her bedroom. She packed her bag and heard the car pull up in the driveway, the car that would take her home, back into the real world. Just as she reached the main living room, suitcase in hand, she heard one of the nuns shouting, "Donna, Donna, come quick, Donna come outside! It's the most beautiful rainbow I've ever seen!"

As Donna rushed outside, she couldn't believe her eyes. In an enormous archway precisely centered over the tree-lined driveway was a rainbow the brilliance of which she had never seen before. The rich golden yellow looked like the sunlit rays of a fountain as it melted into the peppermint green of a mountain, and the crimson red coral and stain of azure purple shone bright like colors in a Persian rug. It was an ethereal masterpiece painted by a heavenly paintbrush, a parting gift of God's love to serve as a reminder of an experience she would treasure forever.

Use the lessons learned in this silent retreat in your own life. "Be still," for in the silence you will feel His peace and know that He is God. "Be still," and drink in the magnificence of every detail in nature—the delicate markings of a flower, the song of a bird, the smell of the air, the feel of moss under your fingertips. Feel God's love for you and the joy that this feeling brings into your life and then give of yourselves. Pour out that love to others, and you will experience the eternal round of God's love in harmony with the heavens. And when you see a rainbow, let it be a reminder.

Life shouldn't be something to be endured until the future arrives.

Your present should be filled with enthusiasm. And, it can be if you will embrace it. Don't look to a husband or a child or a friend or your family to make you happy. It is not within their capacity to do so. Your family, of course, will bring you some of your greatest joys, but look within yourself, for there you will find your happiness, your divine center, your spiritual core of inner strength and peace that knows who you are—a daughter of God.

It is easy to look for happiness in other places, but we have everything we need to be happy now. God is your Father, and He gave you all of these incredible gifts before you came to this earth. Within you is your divine destiny, your celestial traits; even smiles and laughter are from heaven. He gave you the ability to cope with trials, to see miracles each day, to trust in Him, and to know that He is there when you pray.

The Ultimate Gift of course is Christ. He must be the focus of our lives. He, and He alone, offers us peace, His Peace. "Peace I leave with you, my peace I give unto you: not as the world giveth, give I unto you. Let not your heart be troubled, neither let it be afraid" (John 14:27).

WORKS CITED

Ban Breathnach, Sarah. *Simple Abundance: A Daybook of Comfort and Joy.* New York: Warner Books, 1995.

Callister, Douglas L. "Your Refined Heavenly Home." *Speeches 2006–2007.* BYU Devotional, September 19, 2006.

Castleton, Tyler, Staci Peters, and Julie de Azevedo. "Joy in the Journey." Trollhaven Music and Deseret Book, 1998.

Cope, Kenneth. "Start Where You Are." On Goodman Family, *Fortress of Love.* Shadow Mountain, 1996.

De Azevedo, Julie. "Make Enough of Me." *Home.* Salt Lake City: Highway Records, 2004. Used with permission of Shadow Mountain Music Group.

Dew, Sheri L. *Go Forward with Faith: The Biography of Gordon B. Hinckley.* Salt Lake City: Deseret Book, 1996.

———"Knowing Who You Are—and Who You've Always Been." *Ye Shall Bear Record of Me: Talks from the 2001 BYU Women's Conference.* Salt Lake City: Deseret Book, 2002, 277–89.

Ensign. Salt Lake City: The Church of Jesus Christ of Latter-day Saints, 1971–2008.

Evening Light Songs: A Collection of Favorite Hymns and Spiritual Songs for the General Services of the Church. Faith Publishing House, 1949.

Eyring, Henry B. *Because He First Loved Us.* Salt Lake City: Deseret Book, 2002.

Gray, John. *Men Are from Mars, Women Are from Venus: A Practical Guide for*

Improving Communication and Getting What You *Want in Your Relationships.* New York: Harper Collins, 1992.

Hales, Dianne, "If You Think We Think Alike, Think Again," *Reader's Digest,* April 1999, 108–12.

Hinckley, Marjorie Pay. *Glimpses into the Life and Heart of Marjorie Pay Hinckley.* Salt Lake City: Deseret Book, 1999.

Holland, Jeffrey R. and Patricia T. *On Earth as It Is in Heaven.* Salt Lake City: Deseret Book, 1989.

Hymns of The Church of Jesus Christ of Latter-day Saints. Salt Lake City: The Church of Jesus Christ of Latter-day Saints, 1995.

Kimball, Spencer W. *Faith Precedes the Miracle.* Salt Lake City: Deseret Book, 1972.

The Latter-day Saint Woman: Basic Manual for Women, Part A. Salt Lake City: The Church of Jesus Christ of Latter-day Saints, 2000.

LaRoche, Loretta. *Life Is Not a Stress Rehearsal: Bringing Yesterday's Sane Wisdom into Today's Insane World.* New York: Broadway Books, 2001.

Maxwell, Neal A. "The Women of God," in *Woman.* Salt Lake City: Deseret Book, 1988.

Milton, John. *Paradise Lost.* New York: Norton, 2004.

Miner, Caroline Eyring, and Edward L. Kimball. *Camilla: A Biography of Camilla Eyring Kimball.* Salt Lake City: Deseret Book, 1980.

Mitchell, Margaret. *Gone with the Wind.* New York: Macmillan, 1936.

Monson, Thomas S. *Be Your Best Self.* Salt Lake City: Deseret Book, 1979.

Packer, Boyd K. *The Things of the Soul.* Salt Lake City: Bookcraft, 1996.

Shubird, Ernest. "Wings of Morning." *Guideposts* magazine.

Stein, Joseph. *Fiddler on the Roof.* Directed by Norman Jewison. United Artists, 1971.

Wells, Robert E. *The Mount and the Master.* Salt Lake City: Deseret Book, 1991
———. "Wonderful Women in My Life." BYU–Hawaii Women's Conference, August 1997.

Williamson, Marianne. *A Woman's Worth.* New York: Ballantine Books, 1994.

Witkin, Georgia. *The Female Stress Syndrome Survival Guide.* New York: Newmarket Press. 2000.

Young, Brigham. *Discourses of Brigham Young.* Selected by John A. Widtsoe. Salt Lake City: Deseret Book, 1941.

Zondervan Pictorial Bible Dictionary. Merrill C. Tenney, editor. Grand Rapids, Michigan: Zondervan Publishing House, 1963.